A True Life

BUSH PILOT'S
MAYDAY

Bush Pilot's Journal Book One

Ken Forscutt

William McAusland s

A True Life Adventure

BUSH PILOT'S MAYDAY

Bush Pilot's Journal Book 1

Ken Forscutt

Copyright © 2007 Ken Forscutt

Published by Kenneth Brian Forscutt Publishing
#65 650 Harrington Rd, Kamloops B.C., V2B-6T7

First Printing - November 2007
Printed and bound in Canada by Hignell Book Printing
Digital Book Works

Cover illustration design and layout by William McAusland
www.artmotive.com/mcausland.html

ISBN 978 -0-9784514-0-0

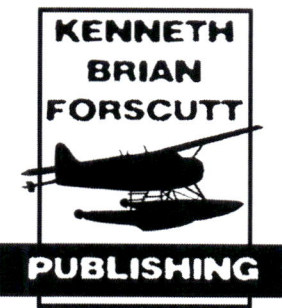

In association with

www.bushpilotsmayday.com

To reorder or find out what other products are available
and go to the above web site. Or contact Ken at
kbfpub@telus.net

Dedication

This book is dedicated to my dear wife, Helen, and to our daughters, Donna and Roberta Lynn. Their total support made it possible for me to complete this book.

Thank you also goes to my dear friend, Marion Williams for her tireless editing and support, as well as the Shuswap Writers' Group of Salmon Arm, B.C., and the Interior Authors' Group of Kamloops, B.C.

A particular dedication goes to the pilots and friends who flew with me enabling this adventure to take place. It is dedicated too, to the aviators who can still navigate with a map and compass!

And lastly, to those pilots who have crossed over to the Other Side and now have God as their co-pilot:

Ken Mulak, Ziggy Wojciechowski, Jim Kehler, Elmer Fossheim, and Dennis Lindsay.

Acknowledgments

The maps of Canada:
Original map data provided by the Atlas of Canada
http:/atlas.gc.ca/ © 2007. Produced under licence from Her
Majesty the Queen in right of Canada, with permission of
Natural Resources Canada.

Marion Williams, editor, Salmon Arm, B.C.

William McAusland, Illustrator, mentor and layout man.
www.artmotive.com/mcausland.html

P in P for their guidance and assistance.

Photos: by Walter Penko, Dennis Lindsay, Helen Forscutt,
Ron Crone, and all the other pilots and friends who submitted
photos.

Preface

I consider myself a lucky man. Two women, two children, and a passion for flying have engaged my soul. My first wife, Ruth, passed away and left me with two little girls; years later, I met and married Helen who has been my best friend and partner for 42 years.

My interest in flying started in 1945 when my brother, Harry, came home from England where he was attached to the R.A.F.625 Squadron. He flew 39 missions over Germany in his Lancaster Bombers by the time he returned home at the age of 21!

It was in 1967 that I got my license and wings at the Brandon, Manitoba Flying Club, and was a whole lot more fun than flying the home-made one out of balsa wood with my dad in the street in front of our house. My first floatplane, CF-HDN was purchased in Snow Lake, Manitoba. And by 1972, my work with the Alberta Government Telephone System brought me to High-Level, Alberta. In 1974 I found myself an active member of the Edson, Alberta Flying Club. But not until an article published in the International Cessna 170B Association magazine [first quarter 1986 addition] was my appetite whetted for writing. At the urging of friends and family I started to write, and even joined a few writing groups along the way.

So here I am 23 years later, retired from the Telus Corporation (a telecommunications company operating in Western Canada) that sent me to the eastern slopes of the Canadian Rockies, including Jasper and the Columbia Ice Fields that I share with you my incredible flying and visual experiences. What I've come to realize is that bush pilots are a dying breed. The use of a compass and map to navigate from point A to point B has been replaced by the GPS (global positioning system) and much more sophisticated navigations aids.

That in itself makes me want to share my experiences. I consider myself a storyteller. And because I have been to places and seen things in the North that many people only dream of, this is my way of letting them see through my eyes. What I hope this book does is light the spark for people interested in flying to believe that they too can achieve their dream. Too many of us have dreams and aspirations that never get filled. This book is a part of mine, and is dedicated to bush pilots and armchair pilots alike.

Northern Friends

It seems their laughter came to me from the
land of the midnight sun.
Tender days, in there sweet ways, to change a
course begun.
We knew not then of life style change; our
off spring's came to be.
We shared with them accomplishments, goals
we would never see.
Emotionally charged we often met, to chart
the course of life.
We often laughed in our firm beliefs, that we
would never judge.

Laughter rings within my ears; Smiles creep
along my face
When assertive words like, "Don't tell me!
Became so commonplace.
Time has come The Creator said,
"to change the black to silver."
My shy, sweet friends will change their lives.
Change their lives forever.

Ken Forscutt
Kamloops, British Columbia
Canada
November 12, 2007

A True Life Adventure

BUSH PILOT'S MAYDAY

Bush Pilot's Journal Book 1

Ken Forscutt

NUNAVUT

Hudson Bay
Baie d'Hudson

CANADA

Lac
Brochet

Churchill

Brochet

*Reindeer
L*

*Southern
Indian L*

Lynn
Lake

South Indian Lake

R Churchill R

Fl Nelson R

Leaf Rapids

Split Lake

Gillam

Shamattawa

Pukatawagan

Nelson
House

Thompson

ONTARIO

MANITOBA

SNOW LAKE

Oxford House

Gods River

Flin Flon

Cranberry
Portage

Cross
Lake

Gods Lake
Narrows

Red Sucker Lake

SASKATCHEWAN

The
Pas

Moose
Lake

*Cedar
L*

Grand
Rapids

Norway
House

Garden Hill

St Theresa
Point

Poplar
River

*L
Winnipegosis*

*L
Winnipeg*

Berens
River

N

Swan
River

Little Grand
Rapids

Bloodvein

Winnipegosis

Fisher
River

Roblin

Dauphin

Ashern

Arborg

Manitoba Map

LEGEND / LÉGENDE

○ Provincial capital /
Capitale provinciale

● Other populated places /
Autres lieux habités

⚜ Trans-Canada Highway
La Transcanadienne

Major road /
Route principale

International boundary
Frontière internationale

Provincial boundary /
Limite provinciale

Ste Rose
du Lac

Fort
Alexander

Russell

Sandy
Bay

*L
Manitoba*

Gimli

Pine Falls

Minnedosa

Neepawa

Portage
la Prairie

Selkirk

Lac du
Bonnet

Virden

Brandon

Beausejour

Scale / Échelle

| 75 | 0 | 75 | 150 | 225 |
| km | | | | |

Souris

Winnipeg

Steinbach

Melita

Carman

Killarney

Winkler

Morris

Sprague

Boissevain

Morden

Altona

Emerson

*Red R
Route R*

CHAPTER 1

The mist was just lifting off the lake as I walked down the dock to my single engine Cessna floatplane. A soft northwesterly breeze created a slight chop on the water that slapped against the plane's aluminum floats. The lonesome cry of Arctic loons echoed across Snow Lake, located some 500 nautical miles north of the city of Winnipeg.

With my left foot firmly planted on the dock I stepped onto the float with my right foot, and, unlocking the door on the pilot's side of the aircraft I placed the keys in the ignition so I wouldn't accidentally drop them into the water. After pumping the floats I noticed the #2 compartment on the passenger's side had about two gallons of water in it. Maybe I had a bad seam or a crack in the aluminium. It was no big deal - most floats leak a little. The oil level on the dipstick indicated it was down about a quart. I added the oil then drained a little fuel from the wing tanks and checked it for water. It was okay. Some gas got on my hands and they tingled as I wiped it off on my floater jacket. But I could still smell that wonderful fragrance of aviation fuel!

Satisfied everything checked okay I untied the aircraft, stepped onto the float and pushed away from the dock. I opened the door, grabbed the door strap and lifted myself into the cockpit. As I did so the aircraft swung around and pointed into the wind. I did my pre-flight tests, switched the master switch to on, pulled the carburetor heat control, switched the magnetos to both, and pushed the throttle control in about a quarter of an inch. I was ready! I slipped on my flying glasses, opened the window and yelled "Clear," and pulled the starter. Suddenly, a detonation cut through the morning air! The airframe shook, the control panel vibrated, the thrashing propeller purred as the engine came to life. The force of thrust started the gyros whining. I adjusted my headset, turned my radio frequency to 126.7 and pressed the transmit button. Taxiing southwest of the government dock for take off in a northwesterly direction, I transmitted "Snow Lake Traffic. Snow Lake Traffic. This is Hotel Delta November.

I heard the static crackle of a voice saying, "Roger H-D-N. We copy. We are at 10,000 due west of Snow Lake inbound for Pukatawagan."

I replied "ROGER H-D-N," pleased to know my radio worked.

I taxied across the lake with the tachometer indicating about 1100 RPM. Small droplets of water danced across the windscreen and rolled along the fuselage. I was headed for a place called Purple Beach, so called because the sand along its shores had a purple tint to it.

When I arrived I nosed my plane into the soft purple sand, shut off the engine, pulled up my knee-high waders and slid off the floats into the clear water. I wanted to check that #2 compartment to see if it had taken on any water. I checked it and everything was okay. I turned my bird around, pulled the water rudders up so they wouldn't dig into the sand, and slid the floats tail first up on the beach. When I climbed into the cockpit and put on my headset I could hear a faint crackling sound. "Oh shit!" I had left the master switch on and the radios were dead. I shut every switch to off, then turned the master switch to on, magnetos to both and pulled the starter. UGH UGH UGH. My battery was too low to start the aircraft.

I knew a small aircraft could always be started by pulling the propeller fast enough to fire the magnetos. Normally, a person stands in front of the prop to do this dangerous little stunt. But on this plane I had to stand on the float on the passenger side, hang onto the cowling, pull the prop down and hope to hell I didn't get chopped into little pieces by the whirling machete! By the way, I had never done this before even

4

in training. All I knew for sure was that once the prop started turning I had to get my hand the hell out of the way!

I slid across the passenger seat and out the right hand door. When my feet hit the float I grabbed the door latch, reached back into the cock pit and set the master switch to on, magnetos to both, and pushed the throttle in part way. I swung around the door and wrapped my arm around the wing strut where there was a small handle riveted to the top cowling in front of the windscreen. It was used to lift you up to the top of the wing to fill the fuel tanks. I found if I hung onto the handle and stretched forward I could reach the propeller. I felt the compression building as I slowly eased the propeller down and moved my hand back. At this point, realizing the position I was in I was scared shitless. This was supposed to be the best day of my life but the sweat was running down my T-shirt and my new flying glasses were sliding down my nose. Remember," Flying is fun. "Flying is fun! "

A crowd had gathered on the dock about a half a mile away so this was no time to turn chicken. Still holding on to the handle, I reached for the prop again and yanked it down as hard as I could. The engine coughed, sputtered black exhaust and then roared. The door slammed shut and my hat blew off from prop wash as the plane pulled away from the shore. I quickly grabbed the wing strut, swung around it and reached for the door handle and gave it a gentle pull. But nothing happened. I tried again, but the door held firm!

I looked down the lake. On the port side the shoreline was about forty feet away. Black rocks topped by spruce trees stretched up from the water. Off to my starboard side were a few motorboats and a small island about a quarter of a mile away. Dead ahead was four miles of open water. A channel ran west along the rocky north shore at the far end of the lake. By now Purple Beach was some five hundred yards behind me where I could dimly see my hat floating in the wake. Well, as you can guess, this was not the way to fly a float plane.

On a Cessna 170B the door lock, a little knob that slides up and down, is located inside the door by the handle. I must have accidentally moved it when I climbed out onto the float. The rudder pedals that steer the plane in the water are attached to a cable, which goes through the firewall and into the cabin. This cable has a ring on it and is placed on a hook inside the cabin after the rudders are pulled out of the water. Without rudders in the water, the aircraft will nose into the wind and keep going. The plane was heading north into the wind and was now about 700 yards from the purple sand. I was soaked from my waist down and getting cold. I knew I must free the cable and lower the rudders, or somehow manage to get that damn door open.

I remembered Irv Kehler, a friend of mine, who had a Cessna, and the window latch on his bird could sometimes be flipped open by striking the door just below the window frame. So I hung onto the strut with my right hand and pounded the door with my left. The window moved a little but did not open. Failing that, I knelt down on the float and grabbed the underside of the engine cowling with one hand and the rudder control cable with other, trying in vain to undo a small bolt that connected the main cable to each float cable. I decided that my only chance was to shake the cable to release it from the hook inside the cabin. On the third try the cable came free. Now I could steer the plane by pulling on the float cables separately.

The Cessna 170 B in take-off mode

Looking up from my soggy perch I saw the north end of the lake coming up quickly. The cables were cutting into my hands and my palms were bleeding. I used every ounce of strength I had to turn the bird around. Now the wind was on my tail and not as much spray was coming from the propeller, but I was drenched from head to toe. I thought I would head back to the beach, gently nose the pontoons into the sand and then start over. About half way back I noticed the pitch of the engine had changed and the thrust was increasing. "Oh shit!" I had forgotten to lock the throttle control. Now the cable was slipping and speeding up the engine. This posed no problem as long as I was going with the wind as there was no lift from the wings, but it would make stopping on the sand almost impossible without damaging the aircraft. Don't forget I had my life savings invested in this plane and had no insurance.

I was approaching the beach too quickly. I noticed the wind had increased to about ten knots straight out of the north and whitecaps were forming on the lake. As I turned the aircraft into the wind the spray from the prop took my breath away. The plane was making a rooster tail in the wake, caused from the prop wash bouncing off the belly of the plane. A rooster tail is the first sign that a float plane will give that it's getting ready to fly.

I had only one choice left. Somehow I must get to the other side of the aircraft, get the door open and gain control of the plane but the waves were making it harder to maintain my balance, and the float rivets were digging into my knees. I stood up and hung onto the wing strut and the handle on the cowling. I looked down the lake and estimated I had about five minutes before I had to turn around again before hitting the beach. I could also see more people had gathered on the dock to watch this fine display of airman ship. Some of the boats were getting closer, but still not too close. I bent over to view the underside of the engine cowling to see if I could shut off the fuel or disconnect the wires to the magnetos. I could see nothing obvious because the water sweeping back from the prop was stinging my eyes. By now I was rapidly approaching the channel and the rocky north shore. Something caught my eye, silver and red. A boat was coming down the channel straight towards me! I hoped he saw me because I couldn't stop, but at the last minute he swerved to the right and headed for shore.

Just then the aircraft started to turn, my port wing lifted and the left float came out of the water as the northerly winds caught the underside of the wing, causing me to nearly tip over. I was very relieved when the airborne float eased itself back to the surface of water. Heading south again, I tried to remember some lesson I may have learned to help me with this predicament. A passage from my Flying Manual came to mind: "Taxiing and steering a seaplane is comparatively easy. One thing must be borne in mind at all times is that there is no way to restrain the forward movement and even though the engine might be throttled right off, there is still sufficient thrust to keep the seaplane moving at a considerable speed! Well they just weren't whistling Dixie, were they?

I came to a decision. I would turn around at the south end and then aim the plane for the widest part of the lake. I hoped this would give me enough time to crawl across the spreader bar onto the other float, get into the cockpit and gain control of this aircraft. It was difficult to maintain good footing as the floats were bouncing in and out of the troughs caused by the one-foot waves. I steered around the island and got a little break from the wind on the lee side. Slowly, I sat down on the float, grabbed the cables with my bleeding hands and brought the aircraft around. Heading into the wind the floats began to porpoise on top of the waves, slowly coming to the surface and beginning to plane across the water. The speed increased rapidly now that the plane was on step. This was my last chance. If I tried to turn again I would probably flip it over.

Kneeling on the spreader bar I pulled myself under the engine and through the prop wash to the other float. As I reached for the wing strut the left float became airborne, then the right. I could feel the wind, no water, just wind, tearing at my face and inflating my cheeks. I grabbed for the wing strut with my left hand and positioned myself to grab the door handle with my right. As I lunged for the door, my right foot slipped off the float, and I slipped backwards. The weight of my body caused the aircraft to bank to the left. The top of a spruce tree scored the back of my neck and a pine cone rolled along the other float then dropped like a bomb. I looked down in horror to see that aluminum boat sixty feet below me.   Never in my wildest dreams, have I imagined I would be caught in this dangerous situation, one day after buying my new airplane.

Chapter 2

Every true-life adventure needs the beginning, and this is where it all began on July 13, 1966.

I strolled towards the hanger with the sign on it that read BRANDON FLYING CLUB. Heat waves bounced off the tarmac like fumes from a gas tank. Tar stuck to the soles of my shoes like toffee to the roof of my mouth. Most of the hanger doors were closed, but one was part way open. I looked through the opening and saw rows and rows of aircraft. There were high wings, low wings, single engine, twin engine, and every make or model imaginable. I walked up close to a canary yellow aircraft with a shiny laminated wooden propeller with polished copper trim. It was a beautiful biplane with two wings on each side, one above the other, and two cockpits, located on the top of the fuselage one for the pilot and the other for his passenger. I could see into the rear cockpit as I stood near the tail section. There was a leather cap and flying goggles sitting on the stick in front of the seat. All that was missing was the white silk scarf!

Suddenly, I turned around as if someone had tapped me on the shoulder to get my attention, but nobody was there. I thought perhaps I shouldn't be near these aircraft, but I was only trying to figure out how they were able to get all these planes into one hanger without banging into each other. Suddenly, I got a whiff of a very peculiar fragrant odour, one I had never inhaled or experienced before. I stood there inflating my lungs and filling my nostrils with this wonderful bouquet. I couldn't place the fragrance, but it was a cross between Hawaiian lei and the shimmering fumes that sometimes tumbled down the fender when my Dad used to fill the gas tank of our old 1932 Essex. I walked out of the hangar and headed towards the flying club office the lingering fragrance from the hangar blended in with the aroma of freshly brewed coffee.

When I entered the office there was a man standing behind a small counter listening to a speaker mounted on the wall. Suddenly the speaker came to life. "Brandon Tower this is Lima, Bravo, November. Over."

Tower: "Lima, Bravo, November, Brandon Tower."

Pilot: "Brandon Tower, Lima, Bravo, November, Ten South, VFR Landing instructions."

Tower: "Bravo, November, Brandon Tower, Runway Zero Eight, Wind One Three Zero at Fife, Altimeter Two Niner, Niner, Two, Cleared to circuit."

Pilot: "Bravo, November."

The man behind the counter nodded his approval and turned toward me and asked, "What can I do for you, young man?"

"I'd like to learn to fly," I said.

"Well, you've come to the right place," he replied. He reached under the counter and pulled out some forms as he kept talking. "What's your name?

"Ken Forscutt."

"Hi, Ken. I'm Len Fisher, chief flying instructor. But first, Ken, you need a medical to apply for your student pilot's license. Okay?" He handed me a royal blue pilot logbook and said, "This is the book we will record your progress as a pilot in." Just then the speaker crackled, making my body tingle with excitement.

Pilot: "Brandon Tower, Lima, Bravo, November on final - Zero eight."

Tower: "Roger Bravo, November, no reported local traffic."

Pilot: "Bravo, November."

I had a smile from ear to ear with excitement, feeling like a soaring eagle high on a thermal lift.

Pilot: "Brandon Tower, Bravo, November down and clear."

Tower: "Roger."

Len smiled and told me the pilot was a student who had soloed just last Thursday and this had been his first long solo flight. "Well, Ken, the cost for a private license is about five hundred dollars and that includes all your books and exams."

I pulled a crumpled fifty-dollar bill out of my shirt pocket and handed it to him. He took it with a smile and said he would put it on my account. Then he looked at his watch and said, "Ken how would you like to go up for a small flip around town to see if you like it?"

"That would be great," I said enthusiastically.

Through the window I saw the young pilot, wearing flying glasses, lock the door on the CF–LBN. When he came into the office Len turned to him and said, "Good radio work, Terry."

"Thanks," he replied. After he left Len continued, "Now, Ken, the plane we will be flying is a Cessna 150 with an indent of Uniform, Delta, Tango or U.D.T."

I don't remember all the checks he did, but the things that stand out in my mind were Len telling me to get in the pilot's seat and buckle up, and then the sound of the speaker in the cockpit and the tower saying, "Uniform, Delta, Tango, cleared for take off on zero eight." The huge zero eight numbers painted on the runway looked as large as the aircraft we were in.

Len told me to place my hand on top of his on the throttle and to follow through with him during take off. The aircraft had dual columns and dual rudder pedals, but the rest of the controls in the aircraft were singular. I had to follow through with my hand on top of Len's hand. His hand moved forward on the throttle control and the panel shook, the RPM gauge indicated 2400, we started to roll and the white dotted line down the center of the runway became a blur. I noticed an upside down two six on the runway below us fade away. We were flying, my very first flight! Wow, what a feeling!

We headed straight west up towards some puffy white clouds. My main recollection at this time was that of another pilot, a 19-year-old pilot who flew Spitfires in 1941. His name was John Magee Jr. and it goes like this:

Oh, I have slipped the surly bonds of earth.
And danced the skies on the laughter silvered wings;
Sun ward I've climbed, and join the tumbling mirth
Of sun split clouds -- and done a hundred things
You have not dreamed of --wheeled and soared and swung
High in the sunlit silence.

Len turned to me and his face broke into a broad grin. When we landed we walked over to the hanger and booked some flight times for the following weekend. That was the beginning of my life as a pilot.

Frank was my first instructor. He taught me to check every nut, bolt and rivet prior to take off. By the way, take offs are easy. I am sure the people who design aircraft teach planes to take off by themselves, but landing on the other hand must have been completely neglected when these birds were built. After about seven hours of instruction my landings consisted of three bounces instead of six. I think Frank thought that my flying would consist of one takeoff for every three landings.

One day, Frank and I had just landed and I was taxiing toward the hanger when he said, "Stop!" I stopped the aircraft to one side of the runway. He started to climb out, but the prop wash caught his cap and it went tumbling off into the grass. He held the door against the wind and said, "Just do everything you learned. Climb out to one thousand feet, do a circuit and land and I will have the coffee ready." He didn't wait for a reply but walked over, picked up his cap and headed for the hanger, never glancing at the aircraft or me again.

13

Well, I had been alone before but never quite like this. I turned the aircraft around and headed for the active runway, knowing everyone in the hanger was monitoring my conversation with the air radio operator to see how much fear was in my voice and to have a laugh at this new pilot. I stopped on the button, did my run up and turned into the wind on the active runway. I slowly closed the throttle, applied a little right rudder, and I was rolling. I watched my RPM, my air speed, and when the airspeed indicated about 50 knots I slowly pulled back on the column and I was airborne. The only thing I could hear was the wheels still spinning after I left the ground. Soon my air speed indicated 80 knots and I started to climb out at 300 per minute. Wow, I was flying! I banked to the left and leveled out at 1000 feet. I had the strangest feeling that someone, or something, was with me that day.

I turned downwind and did my checks, contacted air radio, reported my position and indicated I was about to turn on my base leg, then to my final approach to runway twenty-six. He acknowledged and gave me a new barometric reading and I adjusted my altimeter. There was no other local traffic in the area. I turned onto my final approach, pulled the throttle back and adjusted one notch of flaps. As I started my descent the runway seemed a little smaller than usual. I slowed the aircraft down to eighty knots and waited for the ground to come up to me. My rate of descent was five hundred feet per minute. The telephone poles and buildings soon became life-size again. I leveled the aircraft out and watched my air speed decline. When the wheels hit the runway a small screech was all I heard. I was down and I didn't even bounce! Proud as punch I cleared with air radio and taxied to the hanger, feeling like I had just landed on the flight deck of an aircraft carrier. There was lots of shouting and the customary removal of one of my shirtsleeves. I've never been as proud as when Frank reached up for my logbook, signed in red ink "First Solo" and dated the entry. They say sex for the first time is great. Trust me; it doesn't hold a candle to your first solo flight. For me, this was the beginning, truly the beginning.

YEAR 1966		AIRCRAFT		PILOT or 1st PILOT	2nd PILOT, PUPIL or PASSENGER	REMARKS
Month	Date	Type	Reg.			
						Totals Brought Forward
Aug	9x	CESSNA 150	NPM	F.H. M°MANES	SELF	SEQ 13-14-17 SIM ENG FAIL ON T.O.
Aug	23	CESSNA 150	NPM	F.H.M°MANES	SELF	SEQ 13-14
Aug	23	CESSNA 150	NPM	SELF	SOLO	SEQ 13-14. 1ST SOLO
Aug	24	CESSNA 150	NPM	F.H.M°MANES	SELF.	SEQ 13-14
Aug	24	CESSNA 150	NPM	SELF	SOLO	SEQ 13-14
Aug	25	CESSNA 150	LBN	SELF	SOLO	SEQ 13-14
Aug	25	CESSNA 150	LBN	L. FISHER	SELF	SEQ 13-14 SIM ENG FAIL IN CCT.
Aug	27	CESSNA 150	LBN	L.FISHER	SELF	SEQ 16-17
Aug	28	CESSNA 150	LBN	N.MULIKOW	SELF	SEQ 7,8,9,10,12,17,20,23
Aug	30	CESSNA 150	U.D.T	L. FISHER.	SELF.	SEQ 13-14
Aug	30	CESSNA 150	U.D.T	SELF	SOLO	SEQ 13-14

Total 1st Pilot or Solo		Grand Total (Cols 1 to 10)		TOTALS CARRIED FORWARD
1 Hrs. 55 Mins.		12 Hrs. 30 Mins.		

Ken's logbook with his first solo recorded

Flying itself is not dangerous - it's those damn landings that kill you. I was starting to learn what makes a good pilot. You take fear, mix it with good instruction and competence and the result is a good, safe pilot. Never be too proud to say, "I don't understand," or "Show me again." My instructor once told me there are lots of young bold pilots, but very few old bold pilots.

About thirteen hours into my training I was learning incipient spins. An incipient spin is when the nose of your aircraft is pulled up so it stalls and starts to fall out of the sky. Neat, eh? Well, Len and I were practicing at 6000 feet with a tachometer setting of 1200 RPM. I pulled the nose up and the stall warning sounded, the aircraft shuddered, flipped to the right and started to spin. We recovered and started the procedure again. I asked Len what would happen if this trick were done with cruising speed on. He said to try it, but to take it up to eight thousand feet. So I leveled out at 8000 feet and set the throttle to indicate 2000 RPM and pulled the control column towards my chest. I saw nothing but blue sky. He said pull back harder, but the aircraft kept mushing through the air. Then, finally, when we were almost vertical and the stall warning blaring, the aircraft shuddered, one wing dropped and we flipped over backwards. Dust filled the cabin and we were spinning straight down towards the earth. It looked like a giant checkerboard. This wasn't an incipient spin, this was a full spin, and we were headed straight down completely out of control. The tachometer was red lined. I had no indicated air speed, and we were still spinning straight down. My mouth was dry, my head was dizzy and my arms weighed about a hundred pounds. Finally, Len said, "Get the throttle back and control the spin with your rudders."

I tried to reach the throttle but my right arm felt like it weighed a ton. I managed to get the throttle back and level out the wings. But I was still going straight down with a red line indicating the air speed. Then Len said, "Slowly pull back on the stick so you don't pop all the rivets out of the wings." With the wind ripping past the aluminum skin the noise inside was like a dive-bomber. I finally leveled out at 2000 feet, thirty seconds away from impact with mother earth. My hands were shaking and my T-shirt was soaking wet. When we landed Len turned to me and said, "Never take yours hands off the throttle when you're doing air work. Let's go home."

Still scared shitless, I walked into the hanger and went to the bathroom; afraid I was going to be sick. When I looked in the mirror I saw that my face was as pale as the toilet paper. I came out of the can and said to Len, "That's it. I am not flying anymore. I scared myself today."

"That's funny," he said, "I just booked you for some air work at 13:00 hours tomorrow." He looked over his flying glasses and said, "It's like falling off a horse. If you don't get back on you'll never ride again." That was when he told me he used to be a KLM pilot, which is an abbreviation for the major Dutch airline. Len never told me exactly how he broke both legs in a crop spraying accident, but that was why he had become a flying instructor. I would imagine he was unable to maintain his air transport license with two damaged legs.

16

Order of Proceedings

O CANADA

TOAST TO THE QUEEN

CHAIRMAN — Mr. John Allen

GREETINGS —

THE CITY OF BRANDON
Alderman A. D. Burneski

ROYAL CANADIAN FLYING CLUBS ASSOCIATION
Mr. Andre Dumas, President

Presentations and Awards

GRADUATION CERTIFICATES —
Mr. Frank Hughes, Regional Controller Civil Aviation,
Department of Transport, Winnipeg

PILOT WINGS —
Mr. Len. Fisher, Chief Instructor,
Brandon Flying Club
Mr. Frank McManes, Parade Marshall

H. B. SMITH MEMORIAL TROPHY —
Mr. Alvin Hamilton, Brandon Chamber of Commerce
Winner: Air Cadet W. J. Dawson, Rivers, Man.

CAPT. S.F. DELVES MEMORIAL TROPHY —
Mr. William Turner, Zone Director, RCFCA.
Winner: Bev. C. May, The Pas, Man.

CLUB PILOT OF THE YEAR —
Mr. Andre Dumas, President, RCFCA.
Winner: Air Cadet W. J. Dawson, Rivers, Man.

GUEST SPEAKER —
Wing Commander H. C. Forbell, AFC, CD.

1967 GRADUATES

PRIVATE PILOTS

AGNEW, Neil W.
ANDREYCHUK, Cecil A.
BAHYRYCZ, Andrew A.
BARBER, Brian R.
BARIL, J. Maurice
BINKLEY, Mansel J.
BOOTH, Patrick
BRETSCH, William H.
BROWN, Maynard
BULLOCK, Clayton B.
BUNN, Richard H.
BURNHAM, Robert N.
CAMPBELL, John L.
CHRISTIE, Robert E.
CORBETT, Morley W.
COSTEN, Larry H. G.
COTTINGHAM, David C.
CUMMINS, Val E.
DAWSON, William J.
DITCHFIELD, Glenn A.
DOWD, Ivan L.
DOWD, Murray E.
DOWNEY, James E.
DUNCAN, Thomas S.
DYCK, Richard E.
ELDER, C. Douglas
FETTERLY, Frank L.
FORSCUTT, Kenneth B.
GUNDERMAN, Leslie. H.
HARKNESS, Robert
HAYES, Gerald F.
JERRY-COOPER, Rev. Herbert A.
JEWELL, W. Ralph
JOHNSON, Grant G.

KRUSHEL, L. Walter
KUZYK, Richard D.
LINDSAY, Kenneth G.
MARCH, Robert D.
MARTIN, Murray T.
MAY, Beverley C.
MAZER, Edward J.
MONTEITH, Brian H.
McBURNEY, E. Murray
McKENZIE, S. Arthur
McKINNEY, James A.
McKINNEY, William L.
MERCER, Robert J.
NOTON, G. Douglas
PARKS, Basil W.
PRENDERGAST, John H
RACE, Robert W.
RAMSAY, Vaughn C.
RANDALL, David A.
REID, Douglas H.
REID, Orme W.
RENARD, Desmond G.
SLATER, Blair E.
SPAFFORD, H. Carl
STANLEY, Raymond G.
SULLIVAN, Richard M.
SWANSON, Charles H.
TEICHRIB, John
THOMAS, John R.
TREBOUTAT, Edouard A.
TURESKI, John
WERRY, Edward M.
WILSON, Brian A.
WREGGET, Harvey R.

COMMERCIAL PILOTS

BALDWIN, Mitchell G.
CAMPBELL, Rondon B.
FORMAN, Carl W.
HAITSMA, John
HENDERSON, Lenard W.
HILLIER, D. Keith
LAMB, Terry

MAY, F. Robert
MITCHELL, Walker E.
MUSSELWHITE, David H.
NELSON, Terry L.
RANDALL, David A.
SHUST, Glen S.
WILSON, Arthur

I went back the next day and for several weeks I practiced till I had sufficient confidence to do an incipient spin alone. I still don't like them, but I can still see the look on Len's face when he handed me my wings and my pilot's license. He said with a smile, "Remember, Ken, flying is fun." Many of the pilots I met and trained with went on to careers in aviation. Unfortunately, some died at the sport they loved so well.

CHAPTER 3

I was standing on the dock looking down at the minnows and other small fish swimming around the pilings and the old tires used as bumpers for the float planes that docked here. The sun was warm on my back as I scanned the horizon from the government dock at Snow Lake, Manitoba. I heard the drone of an aircraft in the distance, but I could not yet see it. A small dot in the northern sky, silhouette by cumulus clouds, grew larger. Now the outline of wings and floats were apparent. The noise was very deep and rough. I knew it was not the aircraft I was waiting for because a Cessna engine makes a more purring noise.

When the aircraft, a single engine Beaver, came into full view over the north channel of the lake the pilot extended the flaps one notch and proceeded to land, landing with the wind to save time. He bounced the aircraft once, then twice, and finally slid along the surface on step till he was five hundred yards from shore. He throttled back and the floats sank deeper into the water. He taxied toward me, cut the engine and drifted against the bumpers on the dock. I grabbed the wing strut and held the bird tight against the dock until he could secure it with ropes. It definitely makes it easier when there is someone on the pier when you are docking an aircraft.

Opening his small window the pilot glanced out and thanked me. The rear door opened and two passengers jumped onto the floats to the dock. One lad tied the front ballard of the float to the docking rings while the other passenger tied up the rear ballard. They thanked the pilot and climbed in a waiting company truck and headed for the administration buildings.

When the pilot stepped out of the plane he said "Boy, that's good service."

"I know." I replied.

Then I heard, "Forscutt, what the hell are you doing down here on a Thursday afternoon?"

"I was watching you practice your landings," I said with a grin.

"Don't be a smart ass," he said, and we both laughed.

The pilot, Ron Burgess, was the chief pilot for Hudson Bay Mining and Smelting. We had known each other for over a year, as he was the commercial pilot who had given me my floatplane endorsement on a Cessna 172.

Ron and I stood under the wing of his plane and he said, "So, what are you doing down here on a Thursday afternoon?"

"I'm waiting for my bird," I said.

"What bird?"

"I bought a Cessna 170B with EDO 2000 floats, federal 2500 skis and wheels with heavy-duty 180 gear legs," I replied.

He walked to the end of the dock, then turned and faced me, "You lying bastard. You didn't!"

"I certainly did." I replied. "Look. Here is the certified cheque." I pulled it out of my pocket. When he realized I wasn't bullshitting him he was just about as proud as I was. It obviously gave him a good feeling to know that one of his students had bought his own floatplane.

He reached into the cockpit of the Beaver and pulled out his logbooks. "Come. Sit over here and tell me all about it while I fill out my logbooks." We sat on the edge of the dock and rested our feet on the floats. "So who did you buy it from?" he asked.

"A fellow by the name of Campbell. Ed Hickey is supposed to be here before two pm. so he can catch the bus back to The Pas."

"Well that's neat-o." Ron said. "To bad I can't wait to see it, but I have another flight from Flin Flon to Leaf Rapids at 15:00 hours."

"That's OK. You'll be back again, and who knows? Maybe I'll let you fly it if you promise to practice your landings a little."

Ron laughed, opened his logbooks and asked, "What is the date today?"

"August 26, 1971."

"Time?"

"It's a little after one. 13:06 that is."

He finished his entry in the logbook. "Well, Ken, I'd better get going." He punched my arm saying, "Remember Forscutt, flying is fun."

Smiling to myself as Ron climbed into the cockpit; I untied the aircraft, slipped the rope through the back door and slammed it shut. I walked back to the wing strut and said, "Let me know when you're ready and I'll give you a push."

"Let her go," he called out.

I pushed on the strut till the tail end was clear of the dock. Ron yelled, "Clear" as he fired up the Pratt and Whitney engine. The prop wash was so strong as it accelerated to take-off speed that the wake behind the aircraft formed a rooster tail. Soon he was once more a small dot in the northern sky. By this time I was so anxious that I seemed to hear the sound of float planes every few minutes. Scanning the sky to the southwest, I saw what I thought might be an aircraft but I couldn't hear it. I listened again, but the wind was from the north so any sounds I heard were from the north, not the southwest. Yes, it was an aircraft I could hear, but I couldn't tell what type or what direction it was heading. Then it grew larger and the outline of a floatplane became clear. It headed over the town site, then directly over the dock. The drone of the engine was loud and clear now. As it passed directly overhead I saw the identification under the wing: CF—HDN. It was my bird!

The plane swung to the south end of the lake and landed against the wind like it was suppose to do. As the floats planed across the surface of the water the pilot throttled back and dropped the water rudder down below the floats so he could steer back to the dock. He slid the aluminum float along the tires and I grabbed the wing strut. He popped open the window and said, "Hi Ken, been waiting long?"

"No" I said, "I was talking to Burgess. He just left."
Ed nodded and stepped onto the dock and we tied up the plane. He got out his logbook, locked the door and said,

"That must have been Burgess I heard on the radio."

"Yeah, he left about half an hour ago. Let's go for a coffee and do up the paper work."

"Good idea," Ed agreed.

Ed had to catch the 4:00 pm. bus to The Pas, but before that I wanted to get a checkout ride with him because I had never flown a Cessna 170B. While we were having coffee he signed the certificate of registration and handed me the logbooks and keys. I gave him the certified cheque and as he checked it over I thought of the boat, the skidoo and the travel trailer I had sold to purchase this plane, to say nothing of the loan from the bank. It's hard to believe it cost as much as our first brand new home. Adding to my apprehension was the fact that I had no funds left to buy insurance for my new aircraft.

We drove back to the dock and Ed showed me how to do all the pre-flight checks. When I unlocked the door I noticed a fishing float and a rabbit's foot attached to the key ring. I started to unclasp them but Ed said, "Keep them. There is only one set of keys so if you drop them in the water that float may save you a long walk home." He never did explain the rabbit's foot.

He got out the float pump that was stored behind the pilot's seat and handed it to me. I pumped each compartment on the pilot's side to check for excess water in the air chambers. When I finished he did the passenger side. He told me there was a small leak in the second compartment on the starboard side and I should keep an eye on it as it may have a loose rivet or a stretched seam. He showed me how to push the small buttons up under the wings to drain any water from the fuel tanks. Then we checked the oil and drained the carburetor sump. While I checked the prop for nicks he climbed into the passenger side and buckled his seat belt. I untied the ropes and threw them behind the seat, then pushed with one foot on the dock and the other on the float. Grabbing the strut I placed my foot on the step and climbed into the cockpit.

The cockpit of my Cessna 170 B

I quickly familiarized myself with the instrument panel. After locating the master switch, radio switch, carburetor heat control, magneto ignition switch and throttle control I felt ready to go. Ed warned, "Don't forget to lower your water rudders." I reached up and unhooked the steel ring from the retaining hook and dropped the cable to the floor. I glanced back along the float and watched one rudder disappear below the water. The engine was still warm so I switched the magnetos to both and pulled the starter. The engine roared and the wind blew in the window, cooling the cabin down. I pressed the rudder controls with my feet and watched the aircraft turn to port with my left foot, then to starboard with my right. I taxied across the lake to get a good long run, as this plane didn't have the same engine horsepower as that of a Beaver.

"How do you feel?" Ed asked.

"Just great. A little apprehensive, but just great, "I replied. Then I asked "Are you ready, is your seat belt on, door locked?"

"I'm ready," he replied.

I turned the aircraft into the wind, closed the window, pushed the carburetor heat off, throttle control to full and pulled the control column back into my stomach so the front of the floats rose out of the water. The RPM indicated 2400 and the air speed 40 knots. The aircraft came up on step and started planing across the water. Now that we were planing the air speed rose to 50 knots. I relaxed my grip on the control column and controlled the direction with the rudder pedals, lifted and latched the water rudders and gently eased the column back. One float lifted, then the other. We were airborne! I had "slipped the surly bond of earth."

I headed straight down the lake about fifty feet off the water till the air speed indicated 80 knots. Then I eased back on the control column and climbed out at 500 per minute, up over the trees and leveled out at two thousand feet as indicated by the altimeter. We flew back over the town heading for our house. Helen was standing in the backyard waving a dishtowel, and as I flew over I tipped my wings in salute.

We did a half a dozen "touch and goes" until I was ready to park the aircraft at the dock. After we had secured ropes to the ballards, I drove Ed to the bus station. Since it was 15:30 hours we only had time for a coffee at the Friendly Giant café. As the bus pulled in Ed said, "Ken you have a smile from ear to ear."

I didn't answer. I just kept on smiling. As he climbed up the steps of the Greyhound bus he smiled back at me and said, "Remember, Ken, flying is fun."

The next morning I was trying to sleep but I felt like a kid on Christmas morning. I didn't want to get up too early, but I sure didn't want too get up too late either. Finally, around 7:00 am. I had some coffee and toast, turned the radio on and tuned into the aircraft band, which had been set on 126.7 so Helen could hear me while I was flying. Just then she came out of the bathroom with her eyes at half-mast and said, "What are you doing?"

"Just grabbing a bite to eat," I replied.

"Are you excited?" she asked and I answered, "Does a hobby horse have a wooden dick?" And we both laughed.

She gave me a kiss and said, "Be careful." I nodded and slipped on my floater jacket and out the door I went.

Ken and Helen standing on the floats of their newly purchased aircraft

This is the rest of the story from Chapter One:

I was flying, but just barely above the trees. My rate of climb was too slow and I knew I had to get the aircraft to climb higher to avoid the taller spruce trees along the shore. I needed more power to the engine. Somehow I had to increase the throttle setting. This meant I had to get the door open and reach the throttle control while standing on the float outside the aircraft.

I slowly loosened my grip on the wing strut, transferred

my weight further back on the floats and secured my arm around the step leading to the cockpit. Once my arm was secure I reached up with my free arm to the door latch, unlatched it and wedged my arm between the pilot seat and the passenger seat, then slid my body, head first, between the door frame and the fuselage. I now had my head, both arms, and my upper torso inside the aircraft while still standing on the floats. The air pressure against the door from the prop wash made it very difficult to get inside the plane. I placed one foot on the step, then reached across the seat to the passenger seat and grabbed the cushion and the seat frame and tried to pull myself inside.

Just then my foot slipped off the step, pinning my legs between the door and the airframe, but I managed to wiggle and squirm till my feet were inside the cockpit. I slid the pilot seat as far back as I could so that I could turn around and finally manage to situate myself in the pilot seat. That accomplished, I shut the door and attached my seat belt, applied full throttle and started to climb out at about 300 feet per minute.

When I was at about 1000 feet above the trees I called my wife, Helen, on the radio to let her know I was okay so she wouldn't worry!

Chapter 4

The next few days I spent most of my time checking and cleaning my new aircraft, while assuring my wife that I would not lock myself out of the plane again like on the morning when I went up and down the lake on the outside sitting on the floats. I also needed to get a new battery for the plane. On the weekend of August 30, 1971, Frankie Martin and I flew to The Pas to pick up the wheels, skis, an extra prop and various other parts that went with the sale of the aircraft. We took the rear seat out so we could make room for all the gear. That was my first cross country flight to The Pas, and it was awesome - one of those late August evenings that lets you know winter is just around the corner. The sky was a bright blue with cumulus clouds outlining the earth below. After we radioed into The Pas airport and were given our position we landed on a small lake just west of the airport and north of Clearwater Lake. After we had loaded all the gear we started for home. I know, I know, there is only so much gear and fuel you can put in a Cessna 170B, plus a passenger, before it becomes difficult to take off. I was finally on step, but the shoreline of the lake was coming up fast. I checked my air speed and it indicated about 45 knots. I slowly pulled back on the column and when the plane broke free of the water I lowered the column to build up more air speed just as the floats and the prop hit the cattails at the end of the lake. I eased back on the stick and rose above the willows and shrubs, then radioed the airport and indicated I was on my way home to Snow Lake. I glanced over at Frankie and noticed his eyes were a lot larger then normal. "Boy, the lake didn't seem that small when we landed."

"No, it didn't, did it? " I replied, and we both laughed.

Flying to The Pas I used navigational Omni beacon to guide us over. On the trip home we used maps and a compass, as there were no navigational aids at Snow Lake. It was starting to get dark, the sky had turned from blue to crimson and the moon was full and seemed so close we could touch it. Cool air was forming a mist over the lakes below and it felt like this was a special place in the universe that only Frankie and I knew about. We both sat back and listened to the drone of the engine and watched the mist slowly blanket the smaller lakes and creeks below. The silence was broken when Frankie said, "When will we be home. I have to pee."

I replied, "See the red light in the east? That should be the Snow Lake microwave tower." I estimated about ten minutes and that would be just right as mist and darkness was starting to cover the land.

I kept the tower light on my left and started to descend, turning around the tower and starting my normal approach for the lake. I turned on my landing lights, my navigational lights and the beacon. The flashing red lights reflected off the underside of the wings, casting an eerie glow on Frankie's face. I put on one notch of flaps and peered forward towards the lake. To my amazement there was no lake, just trees and a car on the road with its headlights on. I looked again, circled the tower and realized it was not the Snow Lake tower but the tower at Ponton, thirty miles east of Snow Lake.

I quickly retracted the flaps, applied full throttle and set a heading due west. We had almost run out of daylight. The western sky barely glowed where the sun had sunk below the horizon. It was now dark and I still could not see the Snow Lake tower. As the red glow in the west was a line where the lights should be, I turned on the night flying lamp in the cockpit and glanced down at the map and told Frankie to watch for the red lights of the tower.

We had just passed Wekusko Falls and Herb Lake; therefore I reckoned the tower should be straight ahead. The sky was as black as coal and the stars were popping out all over. Suddenly Frankie yelled, "There's the tower!" Sure enough. There it was. I picked up the top light, then the middle one and slowly banked the aircraft to keep the tower on my left. It was pitch black by now. The stars were bright and the moon was magnificent. I could see the water but the street lights and lights from homes lit up the town below us. I had no idea how I was going to land on water at night with nothing to guide me to the water's surface.

Frankie turned to me and said, "How are you going to land when you can't see the water?"

"I don't know, Frankie. And I have to pee too."

I circled the tower twice and I'm sure every porch light in town came on. I applied one notch of flaps and slowed the aircraft down to 70 knots, flew over our house and there was my dad standing on the back porch waving at his son. He and my mother had come up from Winnipeg for the weekend.

Knowing there was a street lamp on the edge of the lake, I thought if I could fly just over it and start my glide I would be fifty feet above the water. About one hundred yards out in the lake was a small island. Perhaps I could see this as a reference to the water. I started my glide, came over the street lamp and started to flare the aircraft but I couldn't see the island. Too late. I was committed to attempting to reach the water. Just then my landing lights reflected off something. I looked again, and what do you know? It was not my landing lights but the moon reflecting off the water. Ripples danced before me like a well-lit runway. I slid the floats onto the surface and throttled back and the aircraft settled gently into the water.

I turned to Frankie. "I'll turn off the landing lights and you can stand on the floats and have a pee." Which he did. We taxied over to the dock and my dad was standing there, still waving.

When we got home he said, "How did you see to land in the water?"

I smiled at Frankie and said, "I had a great co-pilot and the moon helped too."

Chapter 5

North of Snow Lake, Manitoba.
August 29, 1971.

Gary Zayac, Ron Crone and I were off for a weekend of fishing and hunting. It was one of those fall days when the air
was crisp with frost first thing in the morning and by noon
the smell of wild cranberries filled the air. We left in the
early evening with Ron navigating, responsible for plotting a
course as well as finding a spot to spend the weekend. I flew
low along the tree line, heading north of McLeod and File
Lakes, enjoying the sun as it started to move towards the horizon. I thought we should pick an island with a sandy beach
to set up camp and Ron agreed. Finally, he said, "There's a
good spot. What do you think, Ken?" I flew lower for a better look - nice beach and a small island so no bears. It looked
great. I banked the aircraft, put a notch of flaps and slid onto
the smooth surface of the lake. After we had unloaded the
tents, sleeping bags, food, rifles and fishing gear, I told Ron
to mark the map to show me what island we were on, which
he did. I had to fly back to Snow Lake before dark to pick
up Gary Zayac while Ron set up camp. "Have the coffee on
when we get back," I told him as I got into the plane. I didn't

pay much attention as I taxied out to open water for take off. Turning south towards Snow Lake, something flashed in the western sky like the sun reflecting off a mirror. I glanced below me at the island Ron had marked on the map, where he was now setting up camp. Northern Manitoba must have thousands of lakes, rivers and islands so I wanted to make sure I knew exactly where Ron was.

After landing on Snow Lake, I loaded Gary and more gear and headed back to Ron on File Lake. Flying along, Gary picked up the map and indicated that Ron should be about five minutes away. I checked the map and sure enough this was the island Ron had marked on the map. I started my descent to the small island on the west side of the lake, lowered the flaps and started my final approach. Not seeing any smoke or any signs of life, I flew over the island again and said to Gary, "That's not the island!" I climbed up to about one thousand feet and told Gary to steer while I looked at the map sure enough this was the island that Ron had marked, but it sure wasn't the island where he was. We flew around File Lake and Batty Lake but Ron was nowhere to be found. The sun was getting low in the sky and darkness was approaching fast. I felt a little sick as I said to Gary "Where the hell is he?" I took the map and glanced at all the lakes and islands. I had no idea where Ron was. The sun had started to set when I mentioned to Gary that when I had taken off from the lake I had seen a flash on the horizon.

"Maybe it was a reflection from a forestry tower or a mine shaft," Gary replied.

It was getting darker by the minute as we flew over every island so I put on my navigational lights. Just as I was turning for home, I thought I saw something farther north that looked like a flicker of light on the horizon. I turned north again and there it was - a faint yellow dot on the black lake. It definitely was a fire, but it could be a trapper - or it could be Ron. I flew about five hundred feet above the ground towards the light, maintaining altitude so I could see the contour of the lake. And sure enough! There was Ron on the island. We thought we would teach Ron a lesson so we pretended not to see him. As we flew over the corner of the island he was waving slowly at first, then his arms and red hunting jacket were flailing at the sky as the drone of the aircraft faded away. I'm sure he thought we hadn't seen him. We landed on the far side of the island and taxied back to the beach. I never saw a guy so happy to see an airplane and needless to say I never again let anyone navigate a course without rechecking it

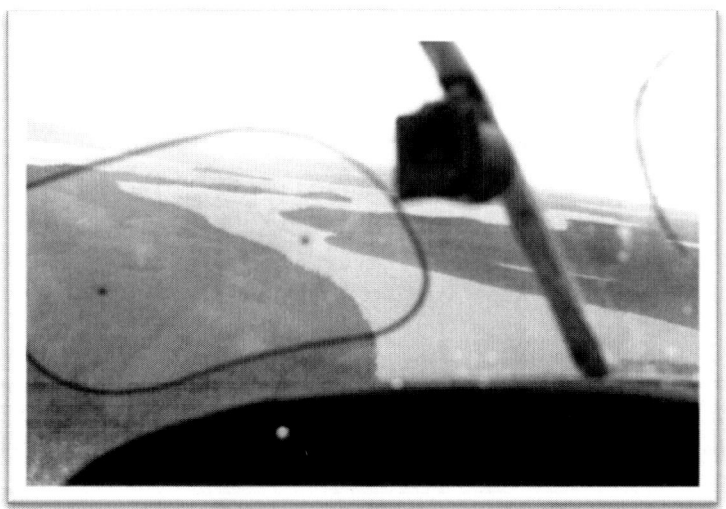

Flying towards an unknown island in the Burnt Wood Lake chain to pick up RonCrone on the distance island

Ken flying towards Batty Lake on a moose hunting trip October 1971

Chapter 6

Batty Lake Moose Hunt.
Hunters: Ron Crone, Gary Zayac, Isaac Reimer, Dennis Hovey, and Ken Forscutt.

This was the major moose hunt of the season. Ron, Gary, and I had often hunted together but this was the first time Isaac Reimer and Dennis Hovey had joined us. The initial plan was to fly Ron and Gary into Batty Lake to set up camp, and then I would go back for Isaac and Dennis.

Ron and I left Snow Lake loaded; there wasn't a spot large enough even for a case of beer. I flew towards Batty Lake, but the weather was closing in fast and ground fog covered the lake completely making it impossible to land. I turned around and headed back towards Snow Lake. It was still early in the evening, but the fog was moving in fast. Ron noticed that

McLeod Lake was still clear and suggested that I drop him and the gear off and ferry the rest of the hunters into McLeod Lake for the night, then we could fly to Batty Lake on Saturday. This seemed like a good idea so I turned north, set one notch of flaps and started to descend to an old trapper's cabin on the west side of the lake. I landed near the half-sunken dock and unloaded Ron and all the supplies. By dark I had all the hunters except Dennis into McLeod Lake. It was none too soon. By the time I had landed and secured the aircraft the lake was covered with a soft, white blanket of fog.

We rose early in the morning to the smell of freshly perked coffee and bacon frying in a cast iron pan. By nine am. I was airborne again with Gary and all the gear. Ron stayed behind with Isaac to clean up the camp. I took Ron in next to help Gary set up camp. I don't think Isaac enjoyed staying alone while I flew Ron in, but I couldn't fly the gear and two passengers at the same time.

We set up camp on a small island about one hundred yards from shore. This was a good place to camp, as we didn't have to worry about bears getting into our food supply. Although we had a small inflatable dingy that would carry two people, a local Indian trapper who lived at Limestone Lake had lent us a twelve-foot canoe that would allow the four of us to hunt from the water two in canoe and two in the rubber raft. To bring the canoe the fifteen miles from Limestone Lake to Batty Lake we lashed the canoe to the outside of floats we inverted the canoe and laid it against the float struts to reduce the drag while we were flying. That made taking off and landing very tricky, but all went well.

The first night we sat around the campfire, drank rum, and called moose. Everything was great until a bellow came from the shoreline and we heard the thrashing of willows. We knew at once that we had called a bull moose down to the water's edge. Gary took his large spotlight to the end of the island but we could see nothing, although we could still hear the splashing and thrashing in the willows.

The next morning just before dawn, Gary took the dingy to the mouth of the creek. I called the moose twice and all hell broke loose. A large bull moose came across the creek heading straight for Gary. He fired his 30-06 once and the moose kept coming. The recoil from the rifle spun the dingy in a circle. Now Gary's back was towards the moose. The dingy kept spinning and each time he lined up with the huge animal he fired, a total of five shots. When the smoke cleared there was Gary still spinning and the huge bull lay dead on the bank. The spread on his rack measured seventy-four inches. Three hours later we had the animal dressed out and hanging in cheesecloth bags in the cool autumn winds. Lunch was a mixture of moose liver and corned beef sandwiches. We were all very tired so we hit the sack early - all but Ron who wanted to try his luck at calling a moose at dusk. He went across the creek and gave a few calls. He thought something answered, but it was getting too dark to see.

The next morning Gary and Ron went back to the creek while Isaac and I cleaned up camp. Suddenly a shot ran out, and then another, it sounded like a shooting gallery. I ran to the edge of the island but I couldn't see Ron or Gary. After an hour had passed I took the canoe and my rifle and went looking for them. There in the willows I saw two orange caps. I yelled, "How's it going?"

They replied in unison "Great. We just shot two yearling bulls." Sure enough there was two young bulls about 100 ft. apart. I went back to camp to tell Isaac that the boys had shot two more moose.

These moose were only about six hundred pounds dressed and a lot easier to handle than the one Gary had shot. We hung the hindquarters over a pole we had strung between two spruce trees. The temperature had dropped to about 19"F and this was great to cool off the meat but it left an icy film on our drinking water. By the time we had finished the sun was just setting over this pristine lake as the loons said goodnight and night sounds replaced their lonesome cry. Well, we had three moose down in two days and it looked like Isaac would break his fourteen-year drought. Wow! Fourteen years hunting and no moose!

I flew back to Snow Lake on October 5, 1971 to pick up Dennis Hovey and bring him back to camp. We hunted for two more days in the best moose country in the world and never fired another shot. This meant Isaac never did get his moose.

On October 8, I flew Isaac and one hindquarter back to Snow Lake. We had a Land Rover at the dock and took the moose to Hans Crone's garage. He was Ron's dad. It took me nine hours of steady flying and hauling to get all the meat back home. I flew back that evening and stayed in camp. I took Ron and Gary out the first trip the next morning and left Dennis to break up camp.

On the way back to Batty Lake I noticed what I thought were two moose wading in a patch of lily pads on a small lake, called Lonesome Lake. I loaded Dennis and all the gear, finished cleaning up the camp and doused the fire. While flying home I told Dennis about the moose I had seen. He didn't believe me, so I flew over the same area but there were no moose to be seen. He said to me "Drop me off and I'll walk past the lily pads to the sandy point."

I said, "OK, and I will fly the gear back to Snow Lake to refuel and come back in two hours." I tried to drop Dennis off on the shoreline but couldn't get too close because of the overhanging trees, so he ended up with wet feet.

Two hours later I circled the area where I had left Dennis, but I couldn't see him. I landed at the sandy point and pulled the aircraft up on shore and waited. Soon I head the crack of willows and the crunching of autumn leaves and I thought here comes Dennis. I grabbed my rifle just in case it wasn't him. The noise came closer and closer, so I called "Dennis."

No reply.

I chambered a shell in my 270 Husquvarna rifle and waited, thinking it might be a bear. Suddenly, about fifty yards along the shoreline, a large black object came out of the willow and walked into the lake. It saw the aircraft, turned back towards the shore and headed straight for me. I shouldered my rifle, placed the cross hairs on its breastbone and fired. It stopped. I reloaded and fired again. It shuddered and kept walking but finally dropped fifty feet in front of the floats. I was still dressing the moose out when Dennis came through the bush. He said he had heard the shots but thought I was just signaling him that I was back. We had the moose skinned, dressed and quartered in no time. It was a good-sized animal as it took two trips to Snow Lake to get the meat out. It was dark when I finally went back to pick up Dennis.

Ken with the moose down northwest of Snow Lake Manitoba

This turned out to be one of our best moose hunts. We were gone ten days and between five hunters we shot four moose. The following weekend I flew back to the Indian trapper's cabin to return his canoe, but he had already gone down the creek and brought it home.

Chapter 7

May 19, 1972
It was a Saturday spring morning when the ice had started to show black patches and the snow cover was almost gone. The sun was warm on my face as we proceeded to load the aircraft. Ron Crone, Gary Zayac and I were off to Woosey Lake, about thirty miles due south of Snow Lake, to do some pickerel fishing before the ice moved out. Some of the best ice fishing takes place at this time of year.

Ken's aircraft on the skis Snow Lake Manitoba

We drove the Land Rover out on the ice and positioned it close to the aircraft wing. In the rear of the Land Rover were two drums of aviation fuel. The drums were very heavy so we tipped them over on the tailgate then rolled them along a plank on the ice. At this time of year water in the fuel will cause the carburetor to ice up, stopping the fuel from getting to the engine. Therefore, we siphoned the fuel through a chamois stretched across a funnel to remove any water. With the tank full and the frost off the windscreen we were ready to go.

Bobbie and Donna waiting for a ski plane ride Snow Lake Manitoba

We slid across the ice like a bobsled. The skis chattered on the cracks in the ice like the tracks on a sled so there was no noise, just the hum of the engine through my headset. We turned southeast into the brilliant sunlight, which instantly heated the cockpit. Gary sat up front in the co-pilot's seat and Ron balanced on two milk crates behind the front seats. Behind Ron were the fishing gear, axe, ice auger and a large white pail to put the fish in.

When we arrived at Woosey Lake we saw smoke coming out of a trapper's cabin on the little river that runs between Ham Lake and Woosey Lake - the area where we wanted to fish. We had to be careful landing on the lake as spring water from the fast- flowing river was melting the ice further out into the main body of the lake. The main part of the lake still had about two feet of good ice, but sometimes on cold evenings water flows over the good ice then freezes. This leaves the lake with a one-inch layer of ice, then one foot of water, then the main body of ice. This type of ice is known as slush ice.

Woosey Lake from the air ice covered with cracks in the ice

When there is snow cover I normally make a pass at the lake, lower the skis down into the snow cover while maintaining flying speed. This allows the weight of the skis to break the top layer of slush ice. When this happens water flows into the ski tracks, which allows you to search out a better landing site.

At this time of year it was difficult to spot slush ice as there was no snow cover and the good ice had a slight film of water on it. We circled twice and the ice looked OK. We started our approach and stayed clear of the open water area. One notch of flap, throttle back, and start to descend. One ski touched, then the other. The aircraft suddenly started to veer to the starboard. I heard a crunching noise then the port wing lifted and the starboard wing crashed into the ice. We pivoted on the starboard wing and came to rest with the port wing pointing towards the sky. One ski was off the ice and fuel was running along my window into the cockpit. The first thing I thought of was fire. The engine stopped. I wasn't sure if I had shut it off or if the prop had jammed into the ice. I shut off the master switch and magnetos and shouted, "Get out!"

I was hanging side wise in my seat, leaning on Gary. Ron was upside down under the milk crates. We couldn't get out of my door, as the fuel would run all over our clothes and into the plane. Gary's door was the only exit. Ron slid his hand along the back seat to the door lock, unlatched it, and pulled up on the handle. The door swung open and rested on the ice. We couldn't see the ski, just a hole in the ice where it had gone through. The wing tip was also under the ice. We weren't sure if we had gone through slush ice or if this was the main ice.

Gary was reluctant to step out to check the ice so we threw out the snowshoes stored behind Ron. When he got out he hung on to the wing strut and stood on the snowshoes, but he didn't sink. Then Ron threw out the milk crates, held onto the strut and stepped out on the inverted crates. He went down about two inches, and then stopped. I slid across the seat, threw out the five-gallon pail, turned it over and asked Ron to sit on it to see how far down it would go. He replied,

41

"Are you crazy? I could go right to the bottom." He was right, but I told him we were in a better position to help him than if I sat on it. Anyway, I didn't want to get wet.

The fuel was starting to make rainbows in the water. Somehow we had to stop it from running out of the wing tank. This predicament put a whole new meaning to John Denver's "Fire and Ice." I had a spare small five-gallon fuel container in the back behind the pilot's seat. When I stepped out onto the snowshoe on the ice I broke through the slush ice, stopping just below my boot tops. I went around the aircraft to the port wing and opened the drain valve. When the container was half full the fuel stopped running.

Now it was time to assess the damage to the aircraft. We found that the right wing tip was bent and jammed up into the aileron. After lifting the wing we were able to right the aircraft. The starboard leg was bent and the bungee cord on the ski was badly torn. We couldn't see the complete ski or the cable fitting as the major part of the ski was under water.

By now we were soaking wet from the knees down and cold. We made our way to the trapper's cabin, taking our lunch and hot coffee with us. The cabin was still warm, but the smell of beaver castors was everywhere. In a few minutes we had a roaring fire going in the old cook stove and soon our socks were drying out. We counted ourselves lucky that no harm had come to anyone. A pilot friend of mine once said, "Any landing you can walk away from is a good landing." I guess this was a good landing.

It was about noon and we had to have a plan of action before nightfall or the plane would freeze in. It was decided Ron and Gary would stay at the trapper's cabin while I went for help. But first we would have to break the slush ice to make a path toward the center of the lake, and then turn the aircraft around, hoping the slush ice would end and then the plane would be on solid ice.

We put on our hot, still wet socks and boots headed back to the aircraft. Ron and Gary packed a path for the aircraft while I took the wing tip cover off as it had been badly damaged. Part of the wing was jammed into the aileron, which meant that I had no aileron movement and would not be able to turn. I took the axe, stood on the five-gallon pail and wedged it between the aileron and the twisted aluminum on the wing and turned it. A gap of about one-quarter of an inch appeared between the aileron and the damaged tip. This should give me aileron control. I tried the control column and sure enough, I had aileron control. I checked the propeller to see if it was bent or broken. It had a few nicks, but nothing serious. The starboard leg was bent, but it looked better now that the aircraft was upright. My only concern was the steel cables that held the skis in an upright position. I reached under the water to feel the connectors and they felt okay, but I wished I could see them. By now Ron and Gary had finished making a path to solid ice. Now, if the engine started and I could develop enough power to push through the slush, I should be able to get airborne.

We drained another five gallons of fuel from the wing tank to make the aircraft lighter for takeoff. I got into the cockpit, started the engine, and checked the aileron movement and rudder control. Everything looked okay except that I was missing the starboard wing tip. And I wasn't sure the bird would fly without it. I told Ron and Gary I would send help as soon as I had radio contact with home.

With Ron on one wing and Gary on the other, I applied throttle and hard right rudder. The aircraft shuddered but didn't move. I gave it more throttle and suddenly it began to pivot on the bad ski. I slowly turned and soon I was lined up on the path the boys had made. I applied full throttle, and as Ron and Gary pushed on the wing struts I started to move. The boys kept pushing and slowly the tail came out of the water and soon I was skimming along the top of the hard ice. I had lots of room so I lifted the plane off the ice then back down, as I wasn't sure how it would perform. Satisfied, I pulled back on the column and rose above the shoreline and spruce trees. I turned back towards the cabin to check on Ron and Gary. They were just about back to the cabin, but I knew they were soaked from the waist down.

Flying north towards Snow Lake note the bent wing on my air-plane!!! It's a little spooky flying with broken wing!

I turned north and headed for Snow Lake. The control column felt heavy and the aircraft wanted to turn to port, which, I thought, was because of the unbalanced wing. Suddenly, there was a loud bang and then another bang. I initially thought of engine trouble, but the instrument panel indicated all was well. Bang! I couldn't see what was wrong but it seemed serious. I banked one way then the other to see if it was associated with the damaged wing tip, but it didn't change. When I tried to locate where the noise was coming from, it seemed to be coming from under the passenger seat. I loosened my seat belt and tried to look out the passenger window. Each time I tried I had to let go of the control column, causing the aircraft to veer to the left, making it impossible to get a good look out the window. I tried to think what could have happened to make the banging noise on the belly of the aircraft. Then suddenly it dawned on me. The ski must have broken loose and was hitting against the fuselage! Fear and panic ran through my mind and body. A cold sweat broke out on my brow. I was about twenty miles south of Snow Lake when this started. Why would the ski break loose during flight? At any rate I knew I was in trouble because I couldn't very well land on one ski and one stubby steel leg. If that leg jammed into the ice, I would flip over.

The only way to get out of Woosey Lake was by rail, or if there was snow, by snowmobile. There wasn't any snow; therefore the only way out was by rail. The only people with a jigger, a motorized work cart used by the game branch and the railway maintenance crews. I radioed the game branch to ask them to go pick up Ron and Gary. They said they would look after it. When I mentioned my situation, they asked if they should call my wife. "No, not yet," I said. "I will get back to you when I get closer to home."

Flying over the Town of Snow Lake to burn off fuel

I climbed up to 7000 feet, up above the puffy white cumulus clouds. I could always think more clearly when I was up there. I needed a good plan. Everything that had happened this morning seemed far in the past. Well, I thought, I could burn off as much fuel as possible; this would reduce the risk of fire if I did flip over. Next, I thought of what I would say to Helen. This was supposed to be an uneventful fishing trip, but it had become anything but non-eventful.

I was playing with the clouds when the fuel gauge indicated it was in the red. I dropped to about one thousand feet over Snow Lake, flew over our house, and then called Gordon at the conservation office. He told me Ron and Gary were on their way home on a CNR work jigger, so that was good news. He asked what I was going to do. I said my fuel was down and I would fly along the open water on the lake and try to land on one ski.

Flying over the Town of Snow Lake and my house afraid to tell Helen of my predicament

I came along the lake, dropped ten degrees of flap, then forty degrees, throttled back till the air speed indicated 50 knots, then 40 knots, applied rudder and aileron so that my left ski touched the ice surface first. My seat belt was so tight I think I cut the blood off to my legs. The starboard leg started to come down lower and lower. There was a bang, a thud and then a grinding noise, but everything stayed upright. The plane came to rest near the government dock and I shut off the engine and switches. My legs were still wet from the lake, but my shirt was soaking wet from sweat. Sitting there, a warm glow spread over me, filling me with a feeling of thankfulness. After an inspection of what I thought was a broken ski, I found the passenger seat belt had been left outside the aircraft and that's what had been banging on the fuselage. Ho Hum. Ho Hum - another non-eventful landing.

Dave Cathcart's twin engine Aztec preparing to fly to Flin Flon
Manitoba November 1972

CHAPTER 8

It's now late fall November 1972. We left High Level aboard a twin-engine Aztec piloted by Dave Cathcart and passengers Alex Patterson, Helen and I. We were going to Flin Flon, Manitoba, to pick up my aircraft, as the wing repair was now complete.

We had moved our family from Snow Lake and were now living in High Level, Alberta. This is a whole other story in itself. We thought we were moving to High River, Alberta, but we wound up in High Level instead. The whole purpose of the move was so the children could get further education in the south. But we had found ourselves back in the north. C'est la vie!

We were now approaching Bakers Narrows, which is Flin Flon's airport about twenty miles south of town, the complete trip from High Level to Flin Flon having taken about three hours. Gary Stubbs met us at the airport and drove us to the aircraft maintenance shop where I could pick up my airplane. The floats had been removed and Federal 2500 fixed skis installed. It was arranged that Dave and I would drive back to Flin Flon and bring the floats out in the spring. The plane was already filled with gas and ready to go. We had arranged that Alex would fly to High Level with me while Dave and Helen flew back in the Aztec. Because the weather was starting to deteriorate we decided we had better head for home. I loaded the survival kit and two Arctic 3-star sleeping bags into the plane. The temperature was about –5 Celsius, and the local pilots had reported that the ice in the bay was thick enough to take off and land on. I watched as a Cessna 185 with hydraulic wheel skis took off on the ice. Then Alex and I taxied to the farthest end of the bay so we would have lots of room before we reached the larger part of the lake where the ice may not be as thick as in the bay. We did our pre-flight check and run up then headed the bird into the wind for take off.

Dave Cathcart as pilot in command in his twin engine Aztec

I checked for local traffic on the radio and announced that I was taking a southwest direction from Flin Flon ski base and would be turning west towards Lac La Ronge, Saskatchewan.

I checked Alex's seat belt and verified the doors were shut and locked, applied full throttle and headed down the lake. The skis chattered across the new ice like someone strumming a tune on a washboard. The tail had started to lift off the ice when Alex nudged my arm and mentioned that the ice out here was really dark and black. I glanced out the port window and suddenly realized that wasn't ice. It was water! Open water about 300 feet deep. I kept full throttle on and told Alex to undo his seat belt and unlock the door. This was in case we crashed he could get out of the aircraft very quickly, and if the door was unlocked, and partially open, it would stop it from jamming into the airframe. We were still maintaining flying speed but I couldn't break the surface tension of the water. I was getting anxious that I would not be able to get airborne. Soon the dead silence of the water on the skis started to make a tick, tick and a thump, thump. I was hitting the pan ice closer to the shore. Then that wonderful strum of the washboard as the harder ice hit under the skis. One wing lifted then the other. We were airborne!

"Yahoo," I shouted. "Alex, do up your seat belt and lock your door."

"Was that water we were over?" Alex asked. When I said it was, he replied, "You know I can't swim."

Although we were aloft the aircraft seemed heavy and hard to control. A little later Alex noticed a large red mine shaft we were heading straight towards, and at our altitude I was right in line with the top of the shaft. I attempted to lift the aircraft above the shaft, but it didn't respond. When I applied the left rudder and then the right rudder, the controls seemed stiff and I was having difficulty moving them. I pressed one pedal then the other and they seemed to work free just in time for us to miss the shaft. We continued to climb to cruising altitude. After climbing to 2000 feet above the ground, I opened my window to check the horizontal stabilizer. I moved the control column back and forth and the rudder peddles to and fro. I realized what was causing my problem was that as we were taking off over the water the spray had frozen on my horizontal and vertical stabilizers. I thought about landing at Baker Narrows but it had a paved runway and I had fixed skis. I needed a frozen lake or an airport with a ski strip and Lac La Ronge had just what I needed.

The overcast ceiling was getting lower, and the odd snow-flake bounced off the windscreen. I mentioned to Alex that if the weather got really bad we might have to put down on a lake and wait out the weather. He replied he wasn't landing on any lake unless we had floats on. So Lac La Ronge here we come!

Five nautical miles from Lac Ronge I notified air radio that I was tail heavy with ice. I also asked. "Do any of the local operators have de-icing equipment?" He said they did and told me which hanger to taxi to.

Starting my final approach to the runway 35, I reduced power to slow my air speed. But as I reduced the throttle, the aircraft stall warning alarm came on. I applied full power, causing me to overshoot the runway. I announced to the radio operator I was tail heavy and required more power to land and that I would be coming in low and fast so the aircraft wouldn't stall. By the way, for those who don't know the word "stall," it means to fall from the sky like a giant rock.

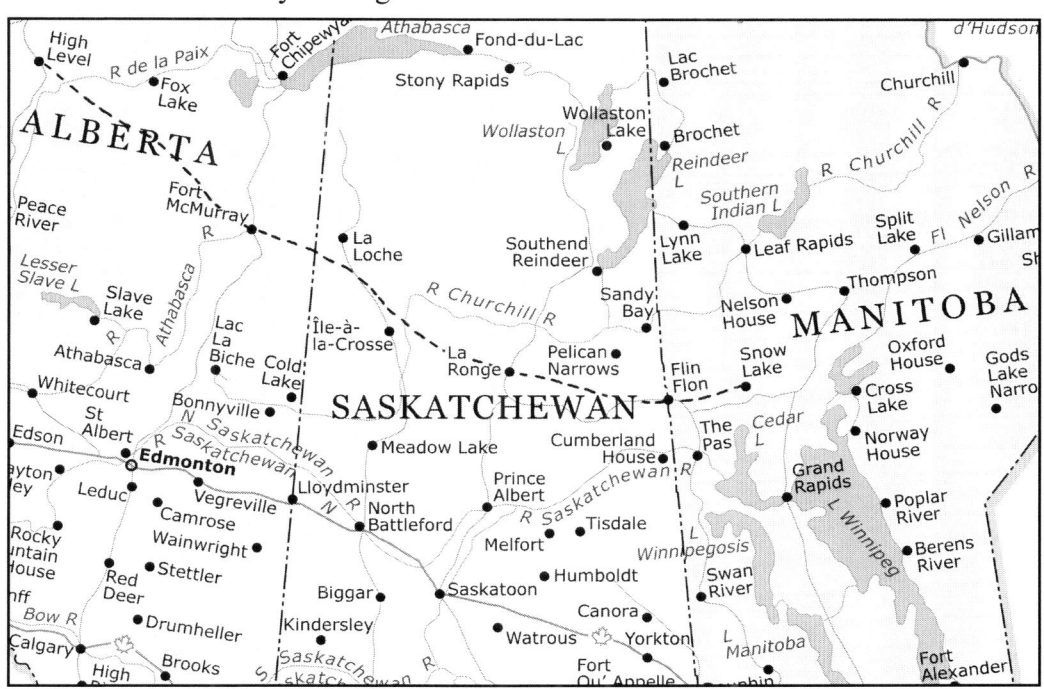

Trip from High Level to Flin Flon took three hours in the Aztec.
Trip from Flin Flon to High Level took three days.

I approached the runway at 90 knots, holding this speed until I was about ten feet above the runway, and then eased the power off. When the aircraft settled into the soft snow I slowly turned it around and headed for the aircraft maintenance hanger. After we had stopped we jumped out to inspect the damage. We discovered half an inch of ice on both stabilizers and the rear part of the fuselage. Just then a mechanic came out and sprayed alcohol on the ice, causing it to melt and fall off in big chunks.

We had left Flin Flon on November 26 at 11:15 and arrived at Lac La Ronge at 13:15 hours. We re-fueled the aircraft and left for Buffalo Narrows at 13:55 hours. With a belly full of gas and a nice clean tail, the aircraft took on a new life. We quickly climbed to cruising altitude and headed for Buffalo Narrows. Alex commented that he was now feeling much better about landing and taking off from airports. The outside air temperature had dropped to −10C with the occasional snow squall which we had to skirt around. By 14:00 hours we were in light snow but we had fair visibility to the ground. Alex was my navigator and he was constantly showing me the lakes that were not frozen over. In retrospect, I think that might have been some sort of message.

Buffalo Narrows had no air radio so I contacted Prince Albert to give them my position and inform them that we would be spending the night at the Narrows. I also asked them to notify my wife that we were okay and should be in Fort McMurray the next day if the weather hung in there. Because the snow had now intensified, I reduced my altitude so that we still had ground visibility. We started across Peter Pond Lake, which was so big we lost sight of the shoreline. The ice was covered with snow except for spots that Alex pointed out that were still not frozen. I continued on a compass heading up to 270° until we picked up the southwestern shoreline, as we had no idea where the airstrip was. We found a temporary strip on the lake outlined with small spruce trees, but Alex was having no part of landing on there. Finally, we found the strip but it was snowing so hard and we couldn't tell if the strip was grass or gravel. Well, here we go. We were about to find out. If it was gravel and there wasn't enough snow on it, with fixed skies we would stop far to fast - if you know what I mean. If it were grass we would slide on the wet snow like a toboggan.

I turned left bank and heard a voice of another pilot heading for Buffalo Narrows in a helicopter. He was having visibility problems and his rotors were picking up ice. I told him we were landing at the town strip and would come to the heliport to give him a hand. As I made the final turn I could still hear the fear in the young pilot's voice. I landed as slowly as possible, hitting the grass but coming to rest on gravel but it was impossible to move the aircraft off the gravel to the side where the grass was. We managed to wave down a local man with a 4 WD truck to tow us off the runway over to the far corner of the grass for our take-off tomorrow.

We asked our Good Samaritan where the heliport was as a pilot was coming in with ice on the rotors and bubble. He said, "Jump in." Then he imparted a piece of local wisdom. "Did you know they send new pilots up north to gain experience and some quit within three weeks and others get sent home in a pine box? Others just keep flying."

We located the pad and we could hear the thump, thump, thump of the rotor blades, but no chopper. Then our friend said, "There he is heading for the ferry. He will be able to find the pad." We kicked as much snow off the pad as we could so he would be able to see the cross. Sure enough, he saw the ferry and turned back and landed on the pad. After he had shut down the engines and climbed out, with a pale smile he said, "It's getting nasty out there. Thank you for clearing the pad."

We needed a room for the night so we asked our friend to drop us off at the hotel. He said he would but not to forget that it was Mary's day off. We didn't quite know what he meant, but we were soon to find out. There was a bell on the desk so I rang it several times. Someone yelled, "It's my day off, we're closed." I said that we needed a room and she replied, "Everybody that comes here needs a room.

Pick a key out of the box and if you need something to eat fix it yourself and clean up the kitchen after." And so we did.

The next morning we left for Fort McMurray about 11:00 where we were told that the snow was light and the weather looked good. The trip from Buffalo Narrows to Fort McMurray was uneventful until it came to landing, as there was no designated area to land a plane with skis. They allowed me to land between the runways but from there I was unable to get to the fuel depot. A man from the Department of Transport driving a small tractor towed me to the fuel pump and back to the grass for the last leg of the trip to High Level, a distance of about 252 nautical air miles.

We left Fort McMurray at 13:55, November 27 and headed northwest. The weather was good, but according to Murphy's Law no weather was reported between these two points. About 45 minutes into the flight the weather deteriorated to less than one mile because of a snowstorm. I decided to head in a more westerly direction to try and get out of the crap, continually reducing altitude to have visual contact with the ground. When visibility became almost zero, and darkness starting to set in, I told Alex to keep a sharp eye out for some place to land. He scanned the ground. "What's that?" he exclaimed. I couldn't see anything but white snow and green spruce trees. After a few minutes Alex exclaimed, "Over there. Turn to starboard." I did a shallow turn, and sure enough I saw smoke coming from a little cabin on the side of a lake. I put on one notch of flap and flew lower over the lake and saw a spruce tree layout of a temporary strip on the lake. Several skidoo tracks pressed the snow down between them. Alex looked across at me and said he didn't want to land on the lake. Knowing how nervous he was I tried to find another spot. I found an old strip north of a few homes. It looked like an old strip and had willows growing out of it. I knew I could land there, but would I ever get out? I flew around the small community for about 10 minutes till daylight was getting sparse. The folks below had skidoos and dogs coming from every which way.

I made up my mind to land on the old strip. I put on full flaps and slowed the aircraft down to 70 knots, then to 60. I touched the snow and sank in the deep white powder completely obscuring the windshield. When the willow boughs slapped the wings and struts it sounded like a drum roll, then they disappeared as the propeller chewed them into bite-size pieces. The aircraft came to rest against a small spruce nestled between the willows. We slid out of our seats into the waist-high snow. I looked at Alex and he had a grin from ear to ear! Just then a skidoo, then another, slid through the willows. The driver parked his machine next to me, slid his goggles over his fur-lined parka and said, "Why didn't you land on the lake strip? The ice is good. The R.C.M.P. landed an Otter on the lake last week."

I said, "It's a long story. Ask Alex."

The skidoos were running up and down through the willows to flatten a path for takeoff. I asked "Should I fly back to the lake to refuel and cover the engine to keep it warm?" They all agreed that's what I should do while one skidooer took Alex and our gear back to the local store. A large dual-track machine was attached by a rope to the tail ski and pulled the plane back to the end of the strip. This allowed the other machines to make a path so I could get a good run through the willows. I asked some kids who seemed to be enjoying all the excitement to hold the rope till I reached full power then let go when I flashed my tail-light.

I revved the engine to 2600 RPM and flashed the tail-light. I shot through the willows and was soon airborne - but none too soon as the willows turned into four-inch spruce trees. After I had circled the lake once I landed between the well-placed spruce trees marking the sides of the runway. I taxied over to the parking area and shut the aircraft down. The villagers soon had the engine covered with a big canvas tarp. They placed an alcohol heater under the tarp to keep the engine warm, as the temperature was –22C.

The only other non-native was the local schoolteacher and store manager. I don't recall his name, but his store was more a trading post and fur station with living quarters. He took us in out of the cold, as Alex and I were wet from the waist down. We dug out some dry clothes from our packs while our host put a couple of logs into the big cook stove. The fragrance in the cabin was a gentle mixture of birch, tamarack, and the exhaust from the coal oil lanterns. His smoke-cured mukluks had to be moved away from the stove so they wouldn't dry out and crack. I'll call our new host Bob, as his real name doesn't come to mind. Bob went into the store and returned with two bottles of some type of liniment. He said, "I want you to drink this with warm water. It's good for chilblains." I had no idea what chilblains were! The bottles contained about four ounces of a brownish liquid. Bob said, "Drink it down and you'll feel a lot warmer." Alex and I placed the small bottles to our lips and down the hatch it went. My eyes started to water and I was gasping for air. Alex reached for a glass of water, but I was faster. I took a gulp, and then passed it to my red-faced friend. To this day I don't know what was in those bottles, but it tasted like Sloan's liniment, Tabasco sauce, and 90 percent pure alcohol. Wow, what a punch! But Bob was right. We weren't cold anymore.

It was important to contact the Department of Transport as our flight to High Level was now overdue and Search and Rescue would be notified that we were missing. Bob had a point-to-point radio and his friend had a receiver and a transmitter so we could try to contact them after supper and get him to relay a message to the Peace River airport. If we got through on this call the airport would notify the Department of Transport, my wife, and Search and Rescue. If the weather was okay, we should be home sometime the next day. The calls were made, and we settled down in the warm and cozy cabin to a wonderful feed of moose stew and bannock. The chinking between the logs had a fragrance of their own - that of something between moose to beaver casters.

We were in the native settlement of Chippewyan Lake where several Indian families lived around the perimeter of the lake. There was a school, a small store and a fur trading station - more than enough to make a man content. Each morning a horse-drawn sled went around the lake to pick up the children for school. Most of the young people spoke English and translated into their native language for their parents. It was a wonderful, hospitable community.

It was getting late and we had a big day tomorrow so Bob, carrying a coal oil lantern, led us to our bedroom. We had our lantern and the bed was turned down. A beautiful four-inch feather quilt was on the bed. We left the door open so the heat from the stove could enter. Bob had been recording some of the native folk tales and he gave me some to read. I will try to relate to some of the stories and describe some of the Indian spirits such as the Windigo, and the story of why beaver and man no longer live in the same lodge.

The native folklore said that man and beavers once lived together in the same lodge and together they would gather berries and branches for the winter months. Man protected the beaver from the wolf, bear, and cougar. The beaver would make dams on the creek to hold back the water and trap fish for man to catch. They lived in harmony for many years until the evil Windigo spirit told man that he could kill the beaver and sell its fur. At first man said no, but the Windigo was persistent and told man he would not have to hunt or fish again. He could trade the beaver pelts for food. So man started to kill the beaver, and the beaver made man move out of the lodge. He was no longer friend to the beaver, and not welcome in their lodge. Man moved out and then the beaver had to warn other beavers that man was bad. So that is why the beaver slaps its tail on the water to warn other beavers when man and other dangers are near. Today, beaver does not like man and they no longer live together in the same lodge. I thought this was a wonderful fable and I enjoy it to this day.

After reading a few more stories, I reached up to blow out the lantern and touched the glass chimney with my fingers. The chimney was very hot and I burnt my fingers, which was very humorous to everyone except my blistered fingers.

The next morning was bright and crisp. Cobalt blue skies were decorated by wisps of pure white smoke going straight up from the chimneys. Bob, Alex, and I walked down to the aircraft. The heater that Bob had placed under the engine had kept the oil nice and warm, but we didn't have sufficient fuel to reach High Level. I asked Bob if he had any aviation fuel he could spare and he replied that he did. He hopped on his skidoo and returned shortly with a ten-gallon drum strapped to the back of his machine. Alex climbed up on the wing and we added the fuel to the starboard tank. I asked Bob what I owed him and he replied, "Twenty-seven dollars, please." This was the most I had ever spent on fuel, but it was godsend.

By now about twenty people had gathered around the aircraft, probably to see what the pilot would do next. A small boy came forward with two tobacco cans, which, they said were for good luck and handed them to me. One can contained lard and the other contained moose jerky. He told me to dip the moose jerky into the lard and eat it like a treat. Somehow I got the impression this boy didn't think we would make it to where we were going. We thanked everyone and said we would return someday then climbed into the aircraft while Bob removed the canvas and the heater. I opened the window and yelled, "Clear" and pulled the starter. The engine came to life. The gang on the lake pulled the tail around with the rope we had attached to the tail ski until we were pointed down the row of spruce trees that had been placed on the ice to mark the runway. I applied full throttle, one notch of flap and took off, tail rope an all. After that, every time I flew with skis on I always tied a rope to the tail ski to remind me of the people of Chippewyan Lake.

When I reached the right altitude I was able to have radio contact with Footner Lake where the airstrip and the air radio at High Level was located. We left Chippewyan Lake at 10:30 November 28, 1972 and arrived at High Level at 13:11 the same day. The adventure had taken three hours to go from High Level to Flin Flon Manitoba, and three days to get home. Upon landing,

Alex was given a Fright Certificate! And I received a Flight Certificate. This had just been another one of those "non-eventful" trips.

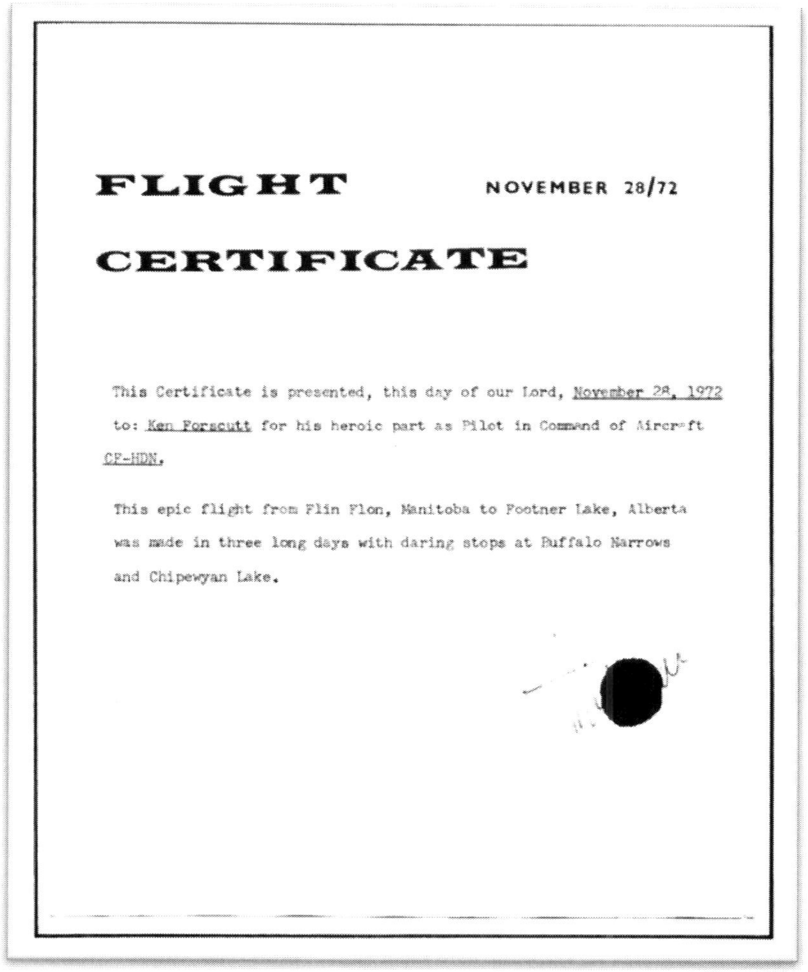

FLIGHT

NOVEMBER 28/72

CERTIFICATE

This Certificate is presented, this day of our Lord, November 28, 1972

to: Ken Forscutt for his heroic part as Pilot in Command of Aircraft

CF-HDN.

This epic flight from Flin Flon, Manitoba to Footner Lake, Alberta

was made in three long days with daring stops at Buffalo Narrows

and Chipewyan Lake.

Photograph of my flight certificate, Alex got one called the fright certificate

Ron and Ken taking off of Footner Lake heading for Fort Simpson in Northwest Territories June the 25th 1973

Chapter 9

North to the Arctic Circle
Trip to the Arctic started in High-Level Alberta and ended out in the Beaufort Sea

Ron Crone and I had discussed flying to the Arctic on several occasions but it was just talk. Everything changed on that day on May 1973 when I phoned him in Calgary and asked him if he would like to fly to the Arctic. He agreed he would, but when I said it would be next month he hesitated for a minute. Ron had been on many trips with me before and this was no small trip. This was a trip to the high Arctic. But he was reassured when I said; "June has the longest days of the year so we would have plenty of daylight."

The journey started on June 25, 1973 from Footner Lake, Alberta, near the town of High Level. This day was one of those special days. The weather was warm, the days long in

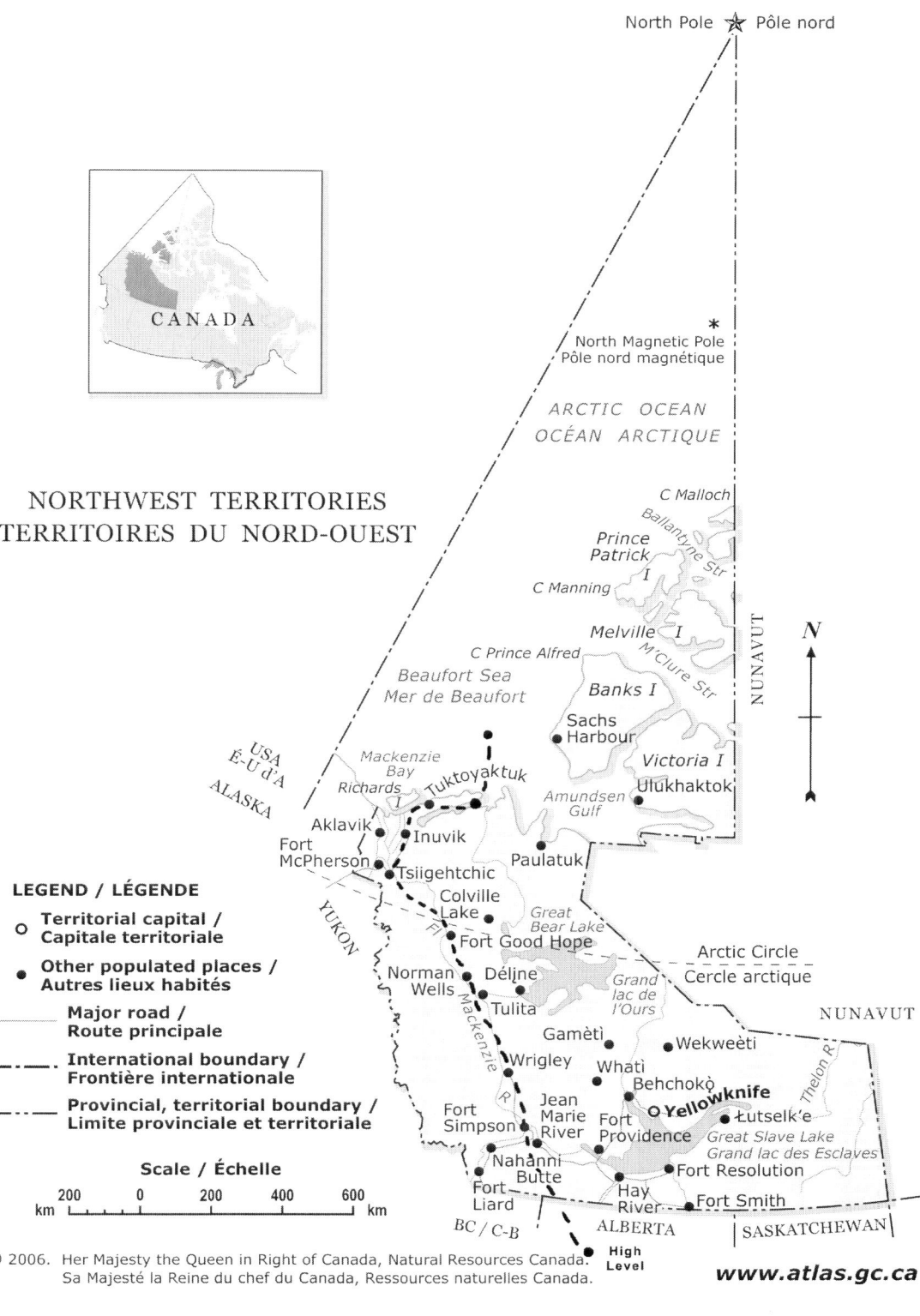

North Pole ⭐ Pôle nord

* North Magnetic Pole
Pôle nord magnétique

ARCTIC OCEAN
OCÉAN ARCTIQUE

NORTHWEST TERRITORIES
TERRITOIRES DU NORD-OUEST

C Malloch

Ballantyne Str

Prince
Patrick
I

C Manning

Melville I

C Prince Alfred

M'Clure Str

NUNAVUT

N

Beaufort Sea
Mer de Beaufort

Banks I

Sachs
Harbour

Victoria I

Mackenzie
Bay

Richards
I

Tuktoyaktuk

Amundsen
Gulf

Ulukhaktok

USA
É-U d'A

ALASKA

Aklavik

Inuvik

Paulatuk

Fort
McPherson

Tsiigehtchic

Colville
Lake

YUKON

Great
Bear Lake

Fort Good Hope

Arctic Circle
Cercle arctique

Norman
Wells

Déline

Grand
lac de
l'Ours

NUNAVUT

Mackenzie R.

Tulita

LEGEND / LÉGENDE

○ Territorial capital /
Capitale territoriale

● Other populated places /
Autres lieux habités

Major road /
Route principale

-·-·-·· International boundary /
Frontière internationale

-··-··- Provincial, territorial boundary /
Limite provinciale et territoriale

Gamètì

Wrigley

Whatì

Wekweètì

Behchokò

Thelon R.

Fort
Simpson

Jean
Marie
River

○ Yellowknife

Ł́utselk'e

Fort
Providence

Great Slave Lake
Grand lac des Esclaves

Scale / Échelle

200   0   200   400   600
km └─┴─┴─┴─┴─┴─┴─┘ km

Nahanni
Butte

Fort
Liard

Fort Resolution

Hay
River

Fort Smith

BC / C-B

ALBERTA

SASKATCHEWAN

High
Level

www.atlas.gc.ca

CANADA

the north, and my best friend, Ron, by my side. We removed the rear seats from the aircraft so we could pack all our supplies, tent, and extra fuel. After attempting to take off several times with no success, we turned back to the dock to remove some gear and lighten the load.

Ron's account was a little different than mine but here is how he remembers it: "When I think back on the day of departure with the water so smooth and we had to leave most of my belongings behind to enable the Cessna 170B to takeoff, I wondered if I should jump ship along with my luggage. As it turned out, this was to be the voyage of a lifetime. The water didn't stay calm for long. The waves started breaking on the front of the floats; the aircraft rose to the top of the waves and started bouncing through the whitecaps. Soon, as we were skimming along the top of the waves, one wing became airborne, then the other wing. The journey had begun. At that moment it was as if someone said, 'they're in the air. Let's let them have it!' A storm tossed us around like a cork in the ocean, but at least it was tossing us in the right direction - north. My dear pilot friend, Ken, had shown me the basics of landing the Cessna on water, for which I was grateful. However, he had failed to mention the fact he had been having a few health problems such as fainting spells. I suppose, in retrospect, it was best I didn't know or he might have been short one co-pilot. So here we were with one pilot subject to fainting spells, one navigator with a sight deficiency, a Cessna 170B with leaky floats, and a newly repaired Automatic Direction Finder, also known as an A.D.F., or navigational radio which detects radio beacons at airports and heads you to their location. Ours quit working thirty minutes north of Footner Lake so we were heading off to God knows where to do God knows what!"

Our first destination was Fort Simpson, North West Territories (N.W.T.) where we required fuel and an updated weather report. We approached with caution as the floatplane base is on the Mackenzie River and I had never landed on a river, let alone a river with very strong currents. We made several attempts to get to the fuel dock, but each time I reduced the throttle the current would drift us away from the dock. Finally,

I came in with a little power and held the aircraft against the fuel dock while Ron pushed the door open got out and secured a line on the floats. When he slipped on the dock and found himself knee deep in the river he accused me of laughing so hard they could have heard me at the North Pole.

Float plane base at Wrigley Northwest Territories

When we landed at Fort Simpson, a remote native village located at the junction of the Laird River and the mighty Mackenzie River, we filled both wings with fuel then took off heading north to Wrigley, N.W.T. We had arranged to have a 45-gallon drum of fuel flown in to Wrigley, as there was no fuel depot there. We followed the Mackenzie River, as we had no A.D. F. to locate the Wrigley beacon. The McKenzie was vast and muddy, as the ice had just broken up some weeks earlier. We passed many barges loaded with food and supplies to service the small communities along its shores. One side of the Mackenzie River is bordered by

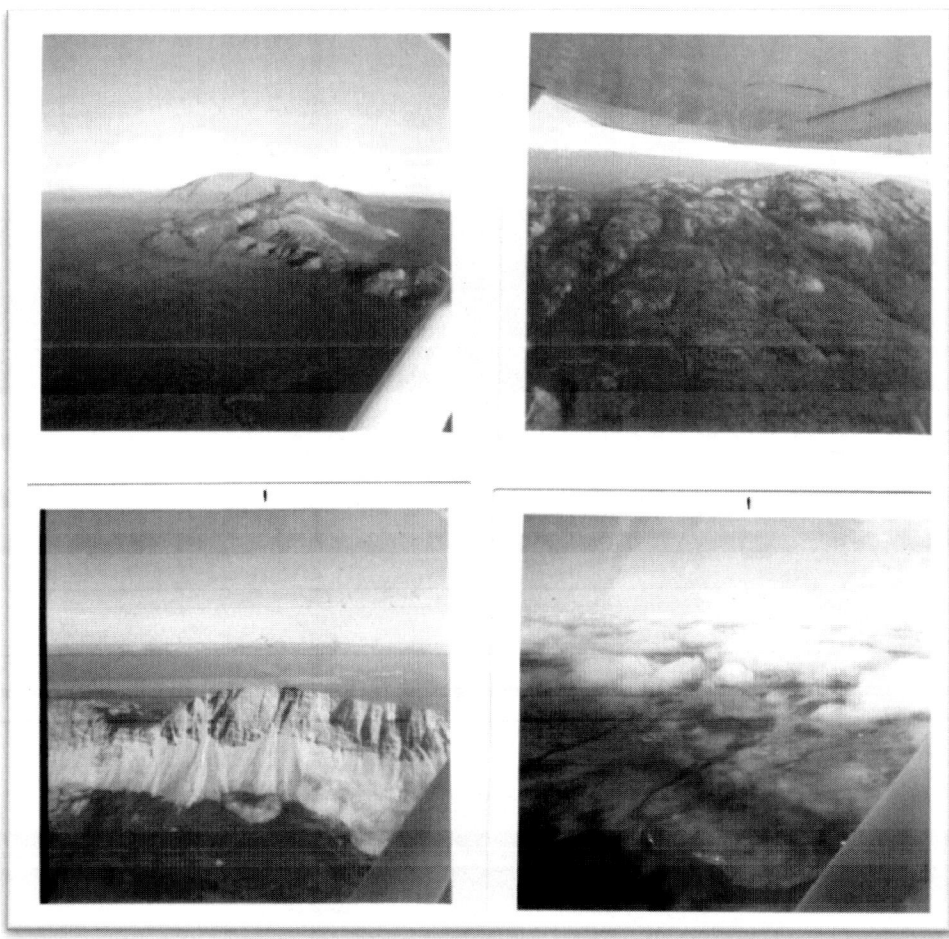

*The McKenzie and Franklin Mountains along the edge of the Macken-
zie River on our way to Blackwater Lake Northwest Territories*

the Franklin Mountains, the other side by the Mackenzie
Mountains. The weather was overcast and the people down
below were undoubtedly hoping for rain as there were many
forest fires burning and the smoke was so bad at times visibility was close to zero. I decided to fly low and just above
the muddy water in case the smoke got so dense we would
have to land. Twenty minutes into this low-level flying the
cabin filled with acrid smoke so that our eyes became ir-
ritated and we were not sure if we had an engine fire or if
the smoke was coming from the forest fires. Soon the cabin

cleared and patches of blue sky appeared on the horizon. It was still stormy, but the skies were clear enough to appreciate the pristine wilderness of the cobalt blue lakes and the Sugar Loaf Mountains. Yes, mountains. I was under the impression the northern part of Canada was a flat nothingness, so what a surprise! The mountains were rounded from the bulldozer action of the glaciers, and then carpeted with soft green foliage right to their peaks. Dotted amongst the green were white dots. I flew closer for a better look. They were sheep, not just any sheep but the famous Dahl sheep.

Fires burning along the Mackenzie River just north of Wrigley Northwest Territories

The clouds and smoke cleared and we continued on to Wrigley. We circled the area a couple of times and landed on a small lake and pulled up to the dock. Within fifteen minutes an old pick-up truck came rambling down the dusty road driven by a bronzed native man with high cheekbones. He gave us a ride to the airport, then loaded the 45-gallon drum of aviation fuel into the truck and took us back to the lake. I offered to pay for this wonderful service, but he refused any payment. But that is the type of hospitality in the north. Ron refueled the aircraft and pumped the floats, while I checked the oil and engine compartment.

Soon we were airborne and headed for Blackwater Lake. This was to be our first overnight stop to do some fishing and just enjoy the non-stop sunshine. We flew around the lake and found a small sandy beach with high cliffs surrounding it. There was a very narrow bay and we made our approach and landed with the wind. Ron's version seems better than mine: "Now landing a small plane is normally a non-eventful happening, but on this trip nothing and I mean nothing, was going to be non-eventful. We had to land with the wind into a bay. There was a big wind and a little bay, and landing with the wind is not a good idea at the best of times. I don't know if I closed my eyes or just blacked out, but after circling around the mountain my next recollection were bulrushes speeding by the window. Now we all know bulrushes grow in shallow water, a place you shouldn't be with an airplane. We skidded up on a sandy beach about four feet from the only tree around and sat there looking at each other; not speaking as I don't think either one of us could have said anything at that point."

Our first night, or was it day, because here the sun never sets so time was suddenly immaterial as if the world stood still and peace and tranquility had entered Ron's and my soul. We found a shallow, fast-flowing river not far from where we had beached the aircraft and soon had camp set up and the coffee pot perking next to the warm fire. While we rigged up our fishing rods with new lines and lures the bet was on who would catch the first fish and who would catch the larges

Ron Crone cooking a feed of Arctic Grayling for our 5 AM supper

The fishing was so great we could have left the lures at home. The grayling or bluefish as the locals call them, hit on anything we cast into the rapids. On one occasion a wild rose petal proved very successful, but so did a plain hook. We released the first thirty, then caught just enough for supper and leaned back on the sandy shores of the river and enjoyed the cool breeze and the warm sun. Mist started to form in the undergrowth and a crimson sky tinged with amber reflected off the mirror surface of the lake. It was almost 5: OO a.m. before we realized we hadn't eaten supper yet. Fried fish and pork and beans over an open fire are a gourmet's delight!

We left Blackwater Lake after a couple of days - or nights. It is hard to keep track of time when the sun never sets. We pushed the aircraft away from the sand and slipped across the ebony water and soon were airborne. Our next destination was a place called Norman Wells. We planned to refuel there, replenish our oil supply and check the aircraft over, as this was our last stop between here and Inuvik, N.W.T. Our navigational aids had failed earlier on the trip; therefore we required dead reckoning and map reading to get from point to point. We followed the Blackwater River to a point where it intersected with the Mackenzie River. Following the mighty Mackenzie River we reached Norman Wells on June 29, 1973. After replenishing our food supplies, fuel, oil, and the ever-present chocolate bars, we left Norman Wells and followed the Mackenzie River over to great Bear Lake, Fort Good Hope, Little Red River and finally to Inuvik. When we arrived we were uncertain where the seaplane base was located. My aircraft was equipped with a VHF radio, known as a Narco VHT 3 super homer. Most pilots called it the coffee grinder because in order to hear the air traffic controller you had to crank the dial around and around while he is counting to get the correct radio frequency. This is a very frustrating procedure if you're attempting to land at a very busy airport. And Inuvik was a very busy airport. We figured there were just as many aircraft landing on this float airstrip as they're probably were landing at the busy Edmonton international airport. Shell Lake is the floatplane base at Inuvik, and the main airstrip was further north. We followed the air traffic controller's directions and made a safe landing, and then he directed us to the fuel docks. We secured the aircraft at the docks, hired a taxi and headed for the local liquor store.

When we arrived at the liquor store we found that they sold rum in 40-ounce bottles. We had never seen anything like these huge bottles of rum. We managed to buy a small fortune worth then headed for the local watering hole, a pub called the Eskimo Inn. We had a nice lunch there and talked to some of the local people. The Inuit people, or Eskimos of the north as they were known then, were very helpful and told us if we wanted to catch Arctic char we would have to fly north to a place called Eskimo Lakes. Or we could fly northeast to a place called Coppermine, as there was a great river there that always had Arctic char. After some discussion we decided to head for Eskimo Lakes and spend three or four days there and then head out to the open ocean known as the Beaufort Sea. Don't forget, although we had a coffee grinder radio we had no navigational aids nor the greatest of maps! What the hell, we hadn't thought we would make it this far but here we were in Inuvik in a pub having lunch and meeting some of the most interesting people of the north.

We couldn't help but notice the bronzed, happy faces of the Inuit children that were in such contrast to the weather-worn faces of their elders. I have wondered at times if the white man's ways have improved the Inuit way of life with our religion, alcohol, and the pursuit of the almighty dollar.

We left that permafrost town and headed north. Where the tree line ended it was if the good Lord had drawn a line in this barren country and placed small trees on one side and frozen tundra and moss on the other. We flew in various directions around the Mackenzie Delta wondering how the people of Aklavik ever found their way in this maze of waterways and islands. Heading north towards Eskimo Lakes we located a small band of caribou grazing on patches of lichens, hidden by the whitish-gray residue of the last winter snow. The aircraft didn't seem to bother the young calves nestled on the dry patches between the snow and the small puddles that had formed. We wondered how this majestic animal could survive in such a hostile environment.

Arctic pingos located north of Tuktoyaktuk natures icebox in the frozen tundra

We continued flying north and noticed that the tundra was changing - small hills were beginning to appear on the skin of this northern world. These hills were frozen tundra pushed up on the horizon like small breasts. These giant frost boils were known in the Inuit language as pingos, which means rounded hill. The center of a Pingo is solid ice. The natives at one time dug holes in them to store their meat, fish and blubber - much like the white man uses his refrigerator. Flying farther and farther north of Inuvik there was no more crackling in my radio. There were no more aircraft. We were alone three hundred miles inside the Arctic Circle. Wow! What a wonderful feeling! We flew north of Eskimo Lakes till we reached the edge of a vast sea of white that we thought was the edge of the polar ice cap then we returned to Eskimo Lakes, which is approximately one hundred miles northeast of Tuktoyaktuk. Ice still covered many places on the lake so we picked a channel that was clear and where the water seemed to be flowing. We circled the area three or four times to make sure there was no debris floating in the water or rocks jutting out from the shore. We started our descent and landed about fifty feet from the shoreline where we found a sandy spot along the edges of the frozen muskeg. I shut the engine down and drifted towards this little open patch. Ron opened the passenger door, got out and ran along the float and secured a rope to the front Ballard. As soon as the float hit the shore Ron jumped off and secured the line. He was no more on shore than the welcoming committee arrived - millions of black flies and mosquitoes. The air was black with them, with a constant drone of insects.

After we had secured the aircraft on frozen chunks of muskeg we went back into the aircraft and opened our backpacks and found our insect repellent. We sprayed, rubbed on and inhaled every type of insect repellent known to man. But this did not deter these ferocious little pests. Finally, we found some repellent used by the Army. It kept the bugs away, but it also melted the plastic frames of our sunglasses. We tried to set up camp, but each time we moved into the soft moss-covered tundra we roused a million new flying insects. Blood started to flow down the back of Ron's neck to his collar. The black flies would make a small red mark and then inject a small amount of anticoagulant, disallowing the blood to flow after their little bellies were full. We covered all parts of our bodies, covering our heads with mosquito nets and tucking our pants into our socks.

We decided it was time to have a nice fresh cup of coffee so I went down to the flowing water and filled the coffee pot and placed it on the Coleman stove. Soon the coffee started perking and soon the aroma of freshly perked coffee filled the air, which seemed to drive the black flies away. We sat on the floats and began to drink the dark brown liquid. After we had both had a mouthful we looked at each other for some degree of pleasure, but there was no pleasure in our eyes. We spat the brown liquid as far as we could! The coffee was salty - very, very salty. It seems you cannot make coffee with seawater. Thinking that these lakes running into the ocean were freshwater lakes was lesson number one. Lesson number two was if you fly into the Arctic you should bring a supply of fresh drinking water! We did not despair for long as we had rum, as well as Coke. We decided that would taste better than any silly old coffee. And while it may not keep the bugs away, we might not care as much.

The next project was to build a fire, make a smudge to keep the bugs away, and then cook our lovely T-bone steaks over an open fire, drink rum and watch the sun that never set. It seemed like a good plan to us, but we were about to learn lesson number three. If there are no trees there is no wood, therefore no driftwood, therefore no fires so we were forced to cook our steaks in a frying pan on the Coleman stove. They were delicious, and so was the rum.

Lesson number four was pretty simple: don't go to the Arctic with a tent that is not self-supporting as the pegs just sink into the tundra. Since we couldn't put up our tent we decided to sleep in the aircraft. We unloaded all the gear and the food, removed the seats and laid our sleeping bags in the cockpit. We put some rum in a Coke bottle and placed it strategically between both of our sleeping bags. After plugging the air vents with pieces of rags and sealing the windows with duct tape, we sprayed the interior with Raid and closed all the doors. After another rum we climbed into the aircraft to dream about fishing the next day. After a couple more medicinal nightcaps, we slipped off to sleep.

When we awoke the next morning, or it could have been the next evening, I had a desperate need to pee, have a crap, brush my teeth and start my day. This was going to be really tricky as we were in bug heaven, and I was afraid a portion of my anatomy was about to be exposed to our buzzing friends. I am sure I was bitten on places on my body that no bugs will ever see again. After a breakfast of bacon and eggs we explored the tundra, lakes and muskeg. We felt for just a moment that we were standing on a shore where no man had stood before. We saw that the north has a wonderful way of co-existing with various species, including man. We found an Arctic fox den not ten feet away from a Canada goose nest with two goslings in it. It didn't seem to bother them to have a fox as a neighbor. The north is a wonderful, wild place. If you ever get a chance to visit this unspoiled area of the world, please go. We fished for a while and caught an Arctic char and ate it raw. We cut thin slices of the orangey flesh, sprinkled them with a little salt and down the hatch they went. It was very good, and to this day I still like sushi and raw fish with a little wasaby, mustard and Soya sauce.

We left the Eskimo Lakes area on June 30, 1973. We flew north of Tuktoyaktuk and headed towards Atkinson Point, over Hutchison's Bay, then out towards the open water of the Beaufort Sea and the Arctic Ocean. We continued in a northwesterly direction and found a spot of open water that was far enough from shore so that we couldn't see land. It wasn't covered with ice so I knew we could land a small aircraft. I slowed the aircraft down to about 70 knots and lowered the altitude till I was about 50 feet off the water. Below me I saw what I thought were two Beluga whales. I set one notch of flaps; throttled back and let the aircraft settle on between the shimmering icy, aqua-blue water.

Ron was not very content when I shut the engine off and allowed all the gyros to wind down so that there was complete silence except for our breathing. This bothered Ron, as I knew my aircraft was hard to start when it was warm. And we were a long way out in the Arctic Ocean. As I stepped out on the floats, Ron opened his door and looked around and broke the silence by saying, "Here come the whales!" I glanced over the fuselage and it occurred to me that I didn't know Beluga whales had black snouts. Then I realized they were not whales but a mother polar bear and her yearling cub! I didn't have to tell Ron to get back into the aircraft as he was already in his seat with his seat belt on. I climbed back in, set the master switch to on, magnetos to both, and pulled the starter. UGH UGH was the response from the engine. My engine didn't start very well when it was hot, and it was hot, and so was I. I tried again. It coughed, sputtered, and then broke into a steady roar. I taxied around the ice floes to find a spot of enough open water for takeoff. I applied full throttle and soon we were airborne. I turned to see if Ron was okay. He was just looking straight ahead without saying a word. Once we were airborne a small smile crept over his face. Then he said, "I thought you said those were Beluga whales." I didn't answer. I just smiled and headed south.

Nanook means white bear in the Inuit language

We flew along the coast towards Tuktoyaktuk, not knowing I was about to learn lesson number five in the Arctic. We were inadvertently flying towards a restricted airspace around the Mid Canada Line Early Warning System at Tuktoyaktuk. Suddenly, a strong authoritarian voice came over the speakers and into my headset. "Aircraft heading 180° at a hundred knots and 30 nautical miles north of Tuktoyaktuk. Please report."

Ron looked at me and said, "Is he talking to us?"

"I think so." I said, and then replied "Hotel, Delta, November, a Cessna 170 B. heading for Inuvik to refuel."

He told us to fly out from the coast and gave us a heading to fly and an altitude to maintain till we were cleared of the restricted air base. He also indicated there was a large fog bank forming off the Oliver Islands and closing in on the Mackenzie Delta. After we were south of Tuk we contacted the control tower at Shell Lake. They also informed me of the large fog bank moving towards the mainland.

We landed on Shell Lake, refueled, picked up six bottles of water and a bag full of chocolate bars. After we left Inuvik we flew in a southeasterly direction to see if we could find a lake that had some good fishing, good water, and firewood so we could have a nice fire and a good cup of coffee. We landed at a lake called Sandy Lake. Why it was called Sandy Lake is beyond me because we flew around the lake several times and there was no sand to be found - just small flat stones that looked volcanic in nature. But the Inuit people called it Sandy Lake, so that was good enough for us. We healed the aircraft up on the black shale, dug out our fishing gear and after three or four casts we had enough trout for our supper.

The mist from the lake soon engulfed our campsite and we consoled ourselves with a few rum and Cokes. Then we climbed into our sleeping bags and buried ourselves in the shale to keep the bugs out, put on our sunglasses and mosquito hoods and slowly slipped off to sleep. While we were still talking the morning air brought with it the drone of black flies and mosquitoes attempting to poke their little fangs into us. We decided we might as well get up and we had a wonderful breakfast of fried trout and bacon. Then we loaded the aircraft and headed in a southeasterly direction to Little Red River, and then on to Wrigley. We landed on the small lake north of Wrigley to refuel the aircraft and camped overnight. The next morning we headed for Fort Simpson.

Fort Simpson has never been my favorite floatplane-landing place because it is at the junction of the Mackenzie and the Liard Rivers. The currents here are absolutely wild, and its murky waters make it very difficult to get to the refueling docks. After jumping in the water and hanging onto the dock, we were able to get a rope on the front of the floats. Finally, we managed to dock the aircraft and fill up both wing tanks, but not before we were soaked from the waist down trying to get to shore. While Ron pumped the floats he shared his chocolate bar with me.

How I managed to taxi away from the dock into the swift currents is still a puzzle to me even today as the current was pushing me into the dock and the wind was coming from a northerly direction. I always try to take off into the wind no matter which way the current comes from. Finally, we had the aircraft on step heading south. We were now on the last leg of our journey to Footner Lake, the floatplane base for the town of High Level, Alberta. We landed on its placid waters on July 2, 1973.

This trip of a lifetime was over - a never-to-be-forgotten experience. There were times when we both thought we might never see our wives and families again, but when we taxied up to the dock they were all there standing in a row waiting for us. No words were spoken between Ron and me.

No words were required!

Chapter 10

Hunting, fishing and flying have always been in my blood, and this was to be one of those trips that every outdoor man would cherish. The date was October 8, 1973. The place was Footner Lake, the floatplane base just north of the town of High Level, Alberta.

The plan was to fly from Footner Lake to the edge of Wood Buffalo national Park, the exact location is a place called Pitchimi Lake where we knew there was an old trapper's cabin and a small wooden dock on the narrow peninsula. The closest neighbors were approximately two hundred miles away. If you call wolves, bears, caribou, and moose as neighbors, then I guess you wouldn't be alone.

Vernon and I had been chosen to go ahead and set up camp at Pitchimi Lake, and then I would ferry the rest of the gang from Margaret Lake into Pitchimi Lake. When Vernon and I took off we had a full load of gear and enough booze to sink a battleship. Because of the limited capacity on the floatplane, we had made arrangements to fly the remainder of our hunting party into a small grass strip at Margaret Lake, giving us a group of four people in the bush for about four days.

When we flew over the grass strip at Margaret Lake, Vernon and I were now about a hundred nautical miles east of Footer Lake. We checked the strip very thoroughly as many aircraft had crashed on takeoff or landing on the soft part of the south end of that strip. Everything looked good so we continued on to Pitchimi Lake. A short while later we crossed the eastern end of Margaret Lake and we could see the outline of Pitchimi Lake on the horizon. The fall frost had painted the tamarack trees a golden color and spruce and aspen provided the yellow, greens, and reds of fall. This was one of those fall days that you can only dream of, flying along at 4000 feet with nothing below you but the fall kaleidoscope and nothing above you but a cobalt blue sky. Suddenly, this beautiful fall landscape turned completely black and a tar-like substance covered the windscreen and the forward part of the fuselage. I couldn't see anything at all so I immediately switched from visual contact with the ground to instrument flying. The artificial horizon is the instrument that tells you that your wings are level and flying straight. The climb indicator and altimeter indicate whether you are climbing or diving, and the airspeed indicator indicates the speed of the aircraft so that you do not stall the aircraft and fall out of the sky.

I attempted to calm my passenger while my heart and my mind raced to figure out what to do, how to do it and what had actually happened. I noticed my oil pressure indicator was slowly dropping and my cylinder head temperature was rising. This was a good indication that I was losing oil. The greatest fear a pilot has is fire. If fire broke out in this aircraft, with all the oil around and no forward visibility, the chance of our survival would be minimum. I slowly monitored all the gauges and said to Vernon, "Everything is okay. Try not to worry."

He looked at me with ping-pong eyes and replied in a very weak voice, "Are you sure everything is OK?"

Now, you realize to land a floatplane you must be able to see, and I had no forward vision. I reached for the mike, pressed the transmit button and said, "Pam, Pam, Pam. This is Hotel, Delta, November. We are presently one hundred nautical miles east of Footer Lake and ten miles south-west of Pitchimi Lake. We have an oil leak and zero forward visibility at this time. We will attempt emergency landing at the first possible opportunity. Please notify the rest of our party not to fly to Margaret Lake until we resolve our problem. There are two souls on board. We have survival gear and at this time no need for search and rescue. Over"

Roger HDN: "Please keep us informed of your situation. HDN. We copy. Footner Lake over and out."

We thought by this time we must be getting close to Pitchimi Lake, but I desperately needed some forward visibility. I slowly opened the pilot's window and found I had good visibility straight down past the floats. Oil was splashing on my flying glasses so I removed them and asked Vernon for a paper towel. I took a small wad of towel and reached through the window and was able to clear a spot on the windscreen about the size of an orange. When I slowly lowered the aircraft to treetop level I could see water below, but I didn't recognize the location. I asked Vernon to pull out the charts and I would try to locate our exact position and radio it back to Footner Lake. I turned slowly with a left bank while I looked out the side window and the small clearing on the windscreen. I had just about completed a 360° turn when I noticed what I thought was a small cabin. I leveled the aircraft off and flew due east trying to keep the cabin in sight. I knew the cabin we planned on using was on a long peninsula, and the bay I would normally land in was long enough but not very wide. I decided to keep the cabin in sight as I slowly lowered my altitude. As we approached the lake I radioed Footner Lake and told them I thought I would be able to land, but once on the water I would not have any radio contact as the line of sight transmission from the lake surface to Footner Lake would be lost. I knew this because of previous attempts from the lake, but if there were other aircraft going over I could relay a message to them and then on to Footner Lake.

The Footner Lake radio operator indicated that Walter, the owner of RKO, a Cessna 180, would fly over the area and make sure we got down okay. I signed off my radio contact with Footner Lake and began my descent. We descended to approximately three hundred feet above the trees. I flew east along the shore, and then turned back towards the cabin and reduced my speed to 80 knots, applied one notch of flap, lowered my speed to 70 knots and looked out the side window until the floats make contact with water. When I saw the wash from the side of the floats I reduced power and pulled back on the column. The aircraft slowly settled into the water but I didn't want to shut the engine off until I was sure where we were. I opened the pilot's door and stood on the floats and saw we were about five hundred yards from the dock. Standing there, I could see small droplets of oil running off the fuselage and hitting the water, forming a million circular rainbows.

I cleaned the windscreen so I had a bigger patch of clear area. I got back into the aircraft, now having good enough visibility to taxi over to the dock and secure the aircraft. After we had docked, Vernon retrieved an old dishpan from the cabin and lodged it under the engine cowlings, as we would probably need this oil to get home. Also, we did not want to pollute the lake. I looked at Vernon, and he seemed a little more relaxed and started to laugh. "Ken your face is covered with oil." Then he exclaimed, "I think we both need a drink!"

Not long after we landed I heard an aircraft approaching from the west. I ran to the dock, activated my radio and contacted it. It was Walter in RKO. I told him everything was okay and he could report to Footner Lake air radio and to our families that we were down and safe. As he was on wheels he was unable to land and provide us any assistance. We requested that he come back the next day and we could better give him an update on our engine problem, but at this time we had no idea what was wrong.

As evening was closing in we decided to build a fire in the cabin, have a drink of rum and start out fresh the next morning. When I returned to the cabin Vernon had a warm fire going in the stove, and as we settled down with our hot rums he said, "What the hell happened? And how long are we going to be here?"

I sipped my rum slowly and replied. "The rest of your natural life, so drink up."

A smile crept across Vernon's face. "You are one crazy bastard."

The next morning we removed the cowlings on the aircraft and cleaned the firewall and the engine with some of the gasoline that we had drained from the wing tanks. Oil was still dripping into the dishpan, but we finally located a hole in the pan just behind the drain plug. We decided to remove the plug and drain all the oil from the engine into some plastic containers we had found lying around the cabin. The oil pan on a 170 B is made up of magnesium, a soft light material, but as I found out later it corrodes very easily and that's what had happened. The oil pan had corroded right through. I cleaned the leaky area and placed a board across the floats so I had better visibility of the hole. When I cleaned the hole out with the blade of my small pocketknife the metal crumbled like sugar into my hand. I continued cleaning it out until I found some good solid metal. The hole was now about half an inch across. We sat and pondered how we were going to plug a hole this large without removing the oil pan. We scoured the cabin from one end to the other looking for a bolt or a large screw or anything that would plug the hole. After two more rums and considerable thought I came up with an idea. If we beveled the hole in the oil pan, then cut a piece from the top of my waders to match the hole, I could place the piece from my waders in the hole and secure it with a willow stick and wedge it against the motor mount. Hopefully, that would make a good enough seal to keep the oil in and allow us to get home.

Vernon said "You've got to be out of your mind if you think I'm going to fly with you with a stick holding the oil in!"

I ignored him and proceeded to find the right kind of branch, green enough to handle the vibration of the engine and strong enough to hold the rubber plug in. It took a full day, one evening, and four rums to complete the task!

The next morning was one of those gorgeous fall days in the North where everything was just perfect. The lake had a small skim of ice on it and the smell of ripe cranberries filled the air. As we walked down to the plane we discussed what to do about the old oil and decided not to use it as it might have small pieces of metal in it. When we had scrounged around the cabin looking for a bolt we had found two cases of snowmobile oil and decided to use that for the lubricant in the engine. We plugged the hole with the rubber plug and held it in place with the willow stick, which we lodged against the motor mount. Then we replaced the drain plug and started filling the crankcase with the snowmobile oil. After we had poured about three quarts of oil in and allowed it to drain down to the crankcase we checked for leaks. Everything seemed okay. We continued to fill the oil pan till we reached maximum on the dipstick. I asked Vernon, if he was ready to fly. He hesitated for a minute and then replied, "No!"

I decided this could be dangerous, so I decided I would take the aircraft out myself. We re-checked the oil one more time, and everything looked okay. I ran the engine up to operating temperature while it was still tied to the dock. This gave us an opportunity to see if there was any oil leaking, and also reduced the risk of fire. Vernon stood on the dock with a couple pails of water just in case there were any problems. I climbed into the cockpit and left the pilot door slightly ajar in case I had to get out of the aircraft quickly. I watched the oil pressure climb slowly on the gauge, and waited for the temperature to start to climb. As the engine heated up smoke appeared from under the cowlings and spread into the cockpit. I felt this was nothing to worry about, as there was still oil on the exhaust manifold that we were unable to reach when we had cleaned the engine. Slowly but surely the smoke started to dissipate. I increased the RPM to 1100, then to 1500 and checked the magneto operations to verify that no oil had got into them. After the engine reached normal operating temperature, I shut it down and climbed out of the cockpit. As the engine was still hot we allowed it to cool down for a while before we started poking around under the cowlings. After about twenty minutes we removed all the cowlings again, checked our rubber plug and the oil drain plug and everything seemed secure and there were no leaks.

We decided to pack the aircraft as light as possible in the event of a crash landing, taking only those things that would help us survive and leaving the remainder of our groceries and anything else behind for a future trip. We took our rifles, fishing gear, three bottles of Scotch, one bottle of rum, and two bottles of rye. As you can see, we only took the essentials! We packed all the gear in the rear of the aircraft, covered it with a plastic tarp and secured it with ropes and seat belts so it would not move in the event of an impact. Since it was now getting late in the day we decided there would not be enough daylight in the event we ran into some problems after take off, so we decided not to leave until the next morning.

Morning came, and there was a feeling of winter in the air. The sky was overcast, the ceiling was about 1500 feet, and there was a strong northwesterly wind. The lake hadn't frozen during the night, but snowflakes had started to fall and the upper portion of the hills that had been golden yesterday was now covered with a blanket of new snow. We loaded the rifles in last. Vernon checked out the cabin while I made one more check on the engine, pumped the floats and made sure everything was ready for take off. As Vernon approached the dock I saw that he had the heel of a bottle of rum in one hand, and a full bottle of Scotch in the other. He looked straight into my flying glasses and said, "If you think I'm getting into that aircraft sober your crazy!" He finished the bottle of rum, and then started on the Scotch. I loaded him in, pushed the aircraft around and pointed it towards the open water and taxied around the bay until the engine reached full operating temperature. I shut the engine down, climbed out on the floats and checked the engine compartment for oil leaks. Everything looked all right, but I had not applied takeoff power and I was unsure of what the vibration would do to my plug if the impact of the floats hitting the waves were to dislodge the willow branch.

Back in the plane, I turned to Vernon to check his seat belt and I asked him if he was ready. He said," No," with a silly grin on his face. I turned the aircraft into the wind, applied full power and one notch of flap and said a small prayer.

The aircraft came up on step, and then the air speed increased to 60 knots. I applied a small amount of pressure on the column. After we were airborne, Vernon turned and looked at me with a little smile of relief. We flew around the lake three times just to make sure everything was working properly, but the oil pressure and temperature remained steady. I attempted to radio Footner Lake, but I was unable to get through.

As I was gaining altitude I noticed snow and rain were starting to turn into ice and forming on the windscreen and the leading edge of the wing. This type of ice is known as rime ice, very rough ice that disturbs the airflow over the wings. As I had no de-icing equipment it was mandatory that I fly lower where the outside air temperature was warmer. I descended to treetop level and continued flying in a westerly direction. I was hoping to contact Footner Lake, but at this elevation I had no chance. The snow was very heavy now, and our forward visibility was less than a mile. Because of the change in the weather I had forgotten all about our instruments regarding our oil leak and oil pressure, so I quickly checked everything and everything seemed okay.

By now I felt we should soon be approaching Margaret Lake. Suddenly, we became engulfed in a fog bank. I eased back on the column to try and rise above it, but as I continued to climb ice started to form on the aircraft so I tried to stay between the fog bank and the freezing rain above me. Vernon hadn't said anything during this ordeal; he just kept sipping on the bottle of Scotch. The trouble we were now in was that we had limited forward visibility, we were unable to go up because of the ice and we had no visibility to the ground. Slowly the fog bank began to dissipate, and we could see the occasional tree and small lake below us.

Suddenly, Vernon said, "What's that?" I peered out the windscreen and saw a huge flock of snow geese straight ahead of us. I managed to avoid the main body of the flock, but two or three of the huge birds bounced off one float and then the other. I had never seen so many geese this close while flying, but I knew many aircraft, even jumbo jets, had been brought down by birds when they had flown into migrating flocks.

We were now above the north Shore of Margaret Lake where I wanted to gain altitude so I could contact the air radio operator at Footner Lake. I climbed till I was just below the clouds and was able to reach Footner Lake and give them my exact position and our estimated time of arrival. This would be the longest part of the trip, as we were about to leave the safety of having water to land on and would be traveling over snow covered spruce trees, muskeg, and mountain ridges. When I saw that Vernon was having a little snooze I reached across his lap and retrieved the bottle of Scotch and had a good snort. The combination of fear, altitude, and alcohol filled my body and soul with a warm glow. We covered the next 120 nautical miles without incident.

Fifteen nautical miles east of Footner Lake I contacted air radio and said I would be flying straight there and asked if there was any opposing traffic. He reported there was none and said he had contacted our wives and families and they would be waiting for us at the dock. I thanked him for all his help and told him I would report on my final approach. I hid the bottle of Scotch, gave Vernon a shake, and started my approach. We landed without incident and taxied over to the dock. The women grabbed the wing and held it firm till I was able to secure the aircraft. Vernon was pretty well loaded by now, and he was unable to get out of the aircraft so I put him over my shoulders and unloaded him like a sack of potatoes. He straightened himself up and, swaying a little, gave me a big hug and mumbled, "You are one crazy son of a bitch!"

*Ed Hunt having his morning wash at Thurston Lake Alberta
along the Alberta and Northwest Territories border*

Chapter 11

I had always talked about my trip to the Arctic in 1972, and each time I told the story more people were excited about my adventure. So in July of 1975 while we were sipping beer at our local watering hole, we decided to fly from Edson, Alberta to Blackwater Lake in the Northwest Territories. All we had to do now was to decide who wanted to go, and how we would make the trip. The six fellows who had decided to go on the trip were Ken Mulak, Ken Biron, Peter Frobel, Ed Hunt, Jim Kehler and I. Since there are far too many Kens for me to keep straight so I will use last names to avoid confusion.

A trip like this required a fair amount of planning. As my floatplane, a Cessna 170 B could handle only two people and a small amount of gear the only way we could accomplish the trip with six people was to take two aircraft. One would be my floatplane, and the other a Cessna 182, which we could rent from the Edson Flying Club. This required a second pilot, and Ken Mulak was chosen to fly the Cessna 182 and I would fly my own floatplane. We had to choose a flight itinerary that would accommodate both planes – a fixed wheeled aircraft that could land on an airstrip, and a lake where I could land. It was decided that on the first leg of our flight I would take off from Bear Lake, about twenty miles north of Edson. Ken would take off from the Edson strip. We would maintain contact using our aircraft radios thereby knowing where each was at any given time. We would join up in High Level where Ken would land, and I would land at Footner Lake, about half a mile from the High Level strip. We would overnight in High Level, then refuel and fly on to Thurston Lake the next morning. Thurston Lake, about six nautical miles from the Northwest Territories border, has a small grass strip and a nearby lake where we planned to do some fishing and check out our camping gear before we went any further north.

The next morning brought with it a gorgeous crimson sunrise, small ripples on Thurston Lake where the whitefish were rising for flies. For a few moments it seemed that we would not have to go any farther north to experience the beauty and the solitude of Canada's northern landscape, not very far from the Northwest Territories border. When Ken arrived we walked up to the runway to meet him and the rest of the gang. After landing, Ken remarked how good the strip was. We walked the length of the strip and discovered that caribou had pounded the grass and clay into a concrete-like base. I knew caribou migrated through this area during the spring and fall, but I wasn't sure where their final destination was. The previous fall I had flown into this area to do some moose hunting, but all we had seen were caribou, hundreds and hundreds of them, but we didn't have a license to hunt caribou, only tags to hunt moose. When we had flown over the strip there were several hundred caribou on it, and about eight wolves milling around at the far end.

We unloaded the 182 and set up camp along the runway. That done Peter, Jim, and Ed went down to the lake to catch some fish for supper. The rest of us built a nice fire. We soon had the cast-iron frying pan filled with pickerel and melted butter. We dipped our bread into the butter and made a pickerel sandwich topped with pork and beans.

Well, the next stop on our trip was Fort Simpson, Northwest Territories. I landed on the Mackenzie River to refuel at the float dock, and Ken went on to another airstrip about twenty miles from the floatplane base. From Fort Simpson, after refueling we flew independently to Wrigley, Northwest Territories, our jumping off spot for Blackwater Lake. With our aircraft radios we were able to keep in constant communication. When Ken arrived at Wrigley he arranged to leave the Cessna 182 at the airport. The manager, Wayne Krueger, lent us his truck to move all the gear and supplies from the airport to the float dock. From there I was to ferry all the guys and the gear into Blackwater Lake, which would take about nine hours flying time, plus refueling. After everything was lined up we decided to camp at the airstrip at Wrigley. The date was June 29, 1975.

Wrigley Northwest Territories June 29, 1975 and the Cessna 182 we had rented for the trip

On June 30, we started to move people and supplies into Blackwater Lake. I spent the whole day loading the aircraft, refueling, and flying along the Mackenzie River to the lake. The nice thing about flying in this country at this time a year is that the sun never sets and you can fly V.F.R., or visual flight rules, all night long. When I finally landed and secured my aircraft on the beach I checked my watch and it was 10: 30 p.m. I had started flying at 8:00 a.m. When I had secured the plane and got to the campsite the gang had supper ready, along with some hot coffee with a little rum in it, which went down very well. We built a fire that danced and crackled long after we had all gone to bed. We kept a fire going for two reasons: to keep the bears away and to stop any wandering moose from trampling down our camp.

Our camp consisted of three tents set in a circle around the fire, which provided both warmth and light during the twilight hours. During the evening, just before we went to bed, we piled green grass and wet wood on it to make a smudge. This kept the mosquitoes and black flies away from our sleeping quarters, but it didn't do much for the smell of our clothing.

The gang I had ferried into Blackwater Lake from Wrigley and fresh lake trout for breakfast

The next morning I woke to the fragrance of perking coffee, bacon, and homemade pancakes. Peter had placed the cast-iron grill over two rocks by the fire, and this made a perfect cooking area. The Blackwater Lake area may not be the most wonderful place in the world, but it's very close to it! Everyone was anxious to go fishing so we put on our waders and headed for the rapids on the Blackwater River. While we were walking along the riverbank we found a partially eaten carcass of a moose. We were unable to tell if it was a wolf kill or had been killed by a bear. Because it was partially covered with leaves and moss it looked more like a bear kill. This type of dead carcass always makes me a little nervous because nothing draws a bear closer to a camp than the smell of meat, particularly bacon, and we had a large slab of bacon in our meat cooler. Peter and I decided to go back to the camp and put the cooler out of reach in a spruce tree and clean up camp.

When we came back to the river Arctic grayling were jumping in and out of the fast-flowing water. We caught enough for lunch, and then decided to do some exploring along the riverbank. Peter was the first to notice it - something white, lying on the bank and covered with branches. We came closer and discovered a small canoe and a paddle. We were all quite excited as we now had a way of getting out into the bay to catch some of the larger lake trout and northern pike.

Since Peter was the most accomplished canoeist in the group, we decided it would be his job to try out the canoe. We pushed him out from the shore and he paddled towards the faster current near the mouth of the river. When he returned he indicated the current was very strong and that we would require an anchor if we were going to fish from this boat. We took some rope from the aircraft, tied it around a fairly large rock and we had our anchor.

Biron was the first out, and he dropped the anchor about a hundred yards from the mouth of the river. He soon had a very large fish on his line and was having difficulty trying to land about a ten-pound lake trout into the very tipsy canoe. After he landed the fish, he slowly lifted the anchor back into the canoe and headed back to camp where he bragged about his catch and took some pictures.

We decided that only one person should go out in the canoe, and under no circumstances was he to stand up in it. We pulled the canoe up on shore and practiced crawling from one end to the other by holding onto the gunnels. Ed said that he wanted to go next as he had never caught a big fish. He was the least accomplished canoeist, and he had a tendency to get very excited. We were all very anxious about him, but he assured us he would be okay. We told him to stay close to the shore just in case! We slowly pushed the canoe out into the lake and soon the current started to pull him and the canoe towards the river. We all said in unison "Set the anchor now!" Ed slowly crawled towards the bow, lifted the rock we had rigged up as an anchor let it slip into the dark blue swirling water. The rope trailed out from the canoe, then tightened, held the canoe for a minute and slipped a little as the rock bounced along the bottom, then finally caught. Ed seemed quite pleased with himself. Once the rope was good and tight he stood up, took two steps and over the side he went!

Ken with another lake Trout and our wonderful deadly white canoe

We couldn't see him as the canoe was upside down. We all called "Ed, Ed, are you okay!" But there was no sign of him. We all had waders on so we held hands and attempted to make a chain to reach the canoe but the water was too deep. We kept calling, and suddenly we heard him calling "Please help me!" We couldn't see him. Where was he? Then we understood that when he had fallen out of the canoe he had come up inside of it! We told him to hang on and we would get to him.

We decided it was too dangerous to use the airplane to rescue him because we couldn't afford to lose our only form of transportation. We convinced Ed to crawl along underneath and untie the anchor rope to allowed him and the canoe to drift towards the shallow rapids in the river. We could see the canoe rocking, but we weren't sure if Ed could untie the rope, as he must very cold by this time. Suddenly, the canoe was moving and heading for the rapids. We ran down the river and formed a line across the shallow rocks until the water was up to our chest. The canoe was getting closer and closer. If we missed him, Ed would be gone! The canoe bounced as it hit the rocks, but we still couldn't see him. Suddenly, the canoe flipped over and there came Ed, bouncing through the rocks like a giant beach ball. I grabbed his shirt, then his belt buckle, then Ken grabbed his leg and we all helped to drag him to shore. He was very, very cold and shivering uncontrollably, obviously suffering from hypothermia and crying hysterically!

We carried him back to the camp, laid him down on the sand by the fire and covered him with a sleeping bag. Then we decided to zip two sleeping bags together, place Ed in the middle, and Peter and I would strip down to our birthday suits, and try to keep him warm. We got him out of his wet clothes and placed him in the sleeping bag. Peter and I climbed in and held him between us until we all fell asleep from exhaustion. When we awoke some three or four hours later Ed was warm, but he was still crying. He said, "I'm so sorry for being so stupid." We assured him, "No worries mate. It was just an accident, and we all make mistakes." We recovered the canoe about half a mile down the river, and, having decided it was too dangerous to use, we placed it back in its storage area.

When Ed was finally warm, as he sipped his coffee I told him I would take him out in the floatplane the next day. This would allow him to fish off the floats, and perhaps get one of those nice big lake trout. He seemed very happy with our new plan. We celebrated his survival with fresh trout, steak, and home fried potatoes - our version of "Surf and Turf".

The next morning we all slept in. Later, because the plane could handle only four people on the floats to fish, we decided to take four out for an hour and then take the rest out after that.

Ed decided not to go out on the first trip, as he was still apprehensive about the water. I taxied the plane out to the middle of the bay and allowed the aircraft to float along with the wind. Fishing from floats can be a lot of fun, but you have to be very careful on how you cast. Because of the antennas, lights, and cables on the aircraft you cannot use an overhand cast. You have to drop the lures straight down off the floats, or cast underhand.

Everyone caught a lake trout or two, the largest about fifteen pounds. I taxied back to camp and picked up the rest of the gang and went back to the same spot where we had had such good luck and repeated the warning about only casting underhand. Ed caught a large lake trout on his first cast, but before we could net it the trout broke his line. After he had retied his line and put a leader on and a six-inch Red Devil lure, I went to the front of the pontoon. I no sooner got set to cast my line when a whistling noise went pass my ear and a searing pain shot through my left cheek! I reached up to see what had bit me and there hanging from my cheek was a brand new six-inch Red Devil lure. You're right. Ed had cast overhand and caught me in the face. I yelled to everyone to stop fishing and stand still. I slowly moved my hand up to the clasp on the leader, opened the clasp and released the line from the lure. Everyone reeled in their lines and placed the fishing rods back in the airplane. We climbed back into the aircraft and I taxied back to camp.

The barb on the hook was deep in the fleshy part of my cheek, the tip of the hook imbedded just under my left eye socket. I held onto the lure as the weight was pushing the second barb deeper under the skin. I sat down on a log while Peter went to get a mirror from one of the shaving kits. When I looked in the mirror I could see what had to be done. The barb had to be pushed through the skin under the eye, being careful not to puncture my eyeball. Once the barb was through the skin, the barb could be cut off and the hook pulled out backwards. I felt I might pass out while this was happening so I lay down on the sand with my head resting on a rolled up sleeping bag. But who would push the hook through? Not Ed, or Ken, or Jim. That left Peter or Biron, Peter tried, but when I winced he stopped. Byron tried, but his hand shook so badly that the barb went side to side, which caused me excruciating pain. They both tried again, but it was no use. They taped the lure to my face so it wouldn't put any more weight on the barb and decided the only thing to do was to fly to the Wrigley nursing station and have it attended to. I took Ken Mulak, the other pilot with me. If I passed out, he could fly the airplane but he didn't know how to land a floatplane!

We left immediately as I was starting to feel Woosey. When we were within fifteen miles from the Wrigley float base I radioed the tower to have someone pick us up at the dock as we had a medical emergency. After we landed a nurse and a driver took me directly to the nursing station. Ken stayed with the aircraft and refueled it in case we had to go to another medical center. In the emergency room I laid down on a gurney and the nurse gave me a shot for the pain and a local anesthetic in my cheek. When the pain was gone she and her assistant proceeded to push the barb and the shaft of the hook through my cheek. I felt no pain, but I sensed the skin on my cheek pulling along the shaft of the hook. Some sort of tool then cut the barb off the end of the hook and the shaft was pulled out back-wards. The wound was cleaned; a disinfectant put on it and dressed with a large padded bandage. After the hook was removed I was given a tetanus shot and told I would not be able to fly the aircraft for at least three hours. They also told me I was very lucky that the hook was brand new and not contaminated or rusty. A vehicle was sent down to the dock to pick up Ken and bring him back to the nursing station to wait with me while I recovered. We arrived back at the camp about 7:00 p.m. that evening. My face was very swollen, and because the freezing was coming out I decided to go right to bed. Ed was very apologetic, but I assured him it was just an accident.

Ken returning back from the Wrigley nursing station still able to fly the float plane

The next morning I awoke to the sound of someone crying outside the tent. I thought it had to be Ed. I unzipped the tent and there he was sitting on a log wearing a bloody white T-shirt. When I got out of the tent I saw that he looked like he had been hit with a chainsaw rather than having just a simple nosebleed. He was covered in blood from the top of his T-shirt right down to the top of his trousers. When he saw me he said, "I got up early to make a nice breakfast for everyone, but while I was chopping firewood a piece flew off the chopping block and hit me on the nose!" I helped him down to the lake, washed his face, took off his T-shirt and stuck two pieces of toilet paper up his nostrils. When we got back to camp he got a clean T-shirt out of his duffel bag and put it on. We teased him while we ate a great breakfast. Ed's face broke forth in a smile like the good trooper he was.

On July 4, 1975 we made preparations to head home, grateful that the weather had been absolutely gorgeous all the time we were at Blackwater Lake. We camped one night at Wrigley before transferring most of the gear to the 182. We left there on July 5 and headed for Fort Simpson where we refueled and then headed on to Footner Lake. The 182 could fly considerably faster than my plane could, so Ken refueled at Footner Lake and headed on to Edson. It was a real pleasure flying in the north at this time of year as we had daylight for 24 hours a day. Peter and I departed from Footner Lake at approximately 7 p.m. and headed directly for Bear Lake, a small lake approximately twenty miles north of Edson where I normally kept my floatplane during the summer months. We had planned to make the four-hour flight directly to Bear Lake with no stops, but as we approached Fox Lake we noticed the sky was starting to darken. I realized that I had made a grave error. There were 24 hours of daylight in the north, but not in the south!

I headed directly for Bear Lake hoping there would be enough visibility to make a landing. I tried to find Shining Bank Lake, which is a much bigger lake where I would have more room to land. I finally located Bear Lake - or what I hoped was Bear Lake. It was about 11 p.m. and many of the people living on the lake had already gone to bed. I flew around what I thought was the edge of the lake, flashed my landing lights and flicked my navigation lights on and off. Suddenly, around the edge of the lake people put on their porch lights and dock lights, and some drove their vehicles down to the beach where I normally kept my aircraft. I could see the beach on the south side of the lake where the homes were, but I couldn't see where the surface of the water was.

Then I noticed two small lights moving out from the beach to where I thought the center of the lake was. I circled the lake one more time, turned on my landing lights, and aimed in the general direction of the first light. I applied one notch of flap and started my descent directly in line with the first light. But I was too high. I applied another notch of flap and reached for the water with the floats. Suddenly a spray came off the float on the pilot side. I reduced the throttle, dropped the flaps and allowed the aircraft to settle in the water. Peter smiled at me and then said, "How did you do that?"

"Just lucky I guess," I replied, "And I had a good co-pilot." We had been home for approximately two weeks when I met Ed's wife at the grocery store. She said that Ed had told her that this was the very best holiday he had ever been on, and he really enjoyed the north! I thought to myself that if this was Ed's best trip, what could his worst trip have been like?

Walter Penko's Cessna 180 CF -RKO with a newly installed engine and ready to head for Pichimi Lake for a week of hunting

Chapter 12

The October days in the north had just settled in and the small bays on Footner Lake had a small skim of ice on them. The tamarack trees had changed from summer green to their fall colors of gold and yellow, providing quite a contrast to the brackish waters of the Lake. The cranberries hidden under the boughs of the tamarack trees had turned crimson red, and some had started to rot producing a strong pungent smell throughout the forest. The spruce trees were still adorned in their summer green and would stay that way throughout the winter.

Walter, Dennis and I had been looking forward to this trip for most of the summer. This day, we loaded Walter's Cessna 180 with our gear and provisions, enough for a week of moose hunting, fishing, and general relaxing in a cabin at Pitchimi Lake. The aircraft had a brand new rebuilt engine and was ready for its first test flight. This was a treat for me as in my 170 B. I would have had to take two or three trips to get all the gear into Pitchimi Lake. Walter, on the other hand, with a Cessna 180 could take three people, and enough gear and booze to look after us for a week. We loaded the sleeping bags and rifles last. Now we were ready to go!

We climbed into the aircraft and taxied to the south end of the lake, did our run up and doubled checked the new engine to make sure everything was okay. When Walter was satisfied with everything that takeoff requires and that the engine was responding properly, he radioed Footner Lake air radio that RKO was ready for takeoff. Air radio reported that there was no a local traffic and he was cleared for takeoff at his own discretion. He turned the aircraft into the wind, adjusted the pitch to full fine, fuel mixture of rich, and slowly applied full power. Soon the floats were plowing through water and slowly came up on step as we skimmed along the top of the waves. The airspeed indicator showed 40 knots, then 50, and went to reach 60 knots. Walter eased back on the control column and we became airborne. We were off to a wonderful adventure at Pitchimi Lake, approximately fifty miles southwest of Wood Buffalo National Park.

When we had climbed to 6000 feet and leveled off, Walter adjusted the mixture control to make the engine run more efficiently at the higher elevation. When he leaned out the fuel the engine began to run very rough and almost stopped! He quickly restored the setting to flow rich and the engine ran normally again. This was very strange, as the carburetor had been replaced when the engine was replaced; therefore this was a brand new carburetor on this engine. We discussed what could be wrong and decided we had picked up carburetor icing on takeoff and should apply carburetor heat before we reduced the fuel mixture. We also decided to try it again over a lake so we would have water under us in case something else failed. We had about twenty-five miles to go to reach the west end of Margaret Lake. We knew there was a lodge about halfway down the north side of the lake, with a small airstrip and the dock for floatplanes. We felt that if we had a problem we could land on the lake and have a mechanic flown in from Footner Lake.

When we had the lodge in sight Walter applied carburetor heat. This procedure takes some of the hot air from the exhaust and passes it through the carburetor to melt away any ice that may have been formed while flying through moist air. He left it on for about two minutes and then shut it off and started to lean out the fuel mixture. All went well so we concluded that we must have had some carburetor icing. We started to descend to a lower altitude as we were getting closer to Pitchimi Lake and Walter returned the fuel mixture to flow rich for our descent. The aircraft punched through some low cloud and fog and we continued dropping to about 200 feet per minute until we had Pitchimi Lake in sight. We flew around the lake and looked for a suitable landing spot in the small bay next to the trapper's cabin that was going to be our home for the next week. The aircraft settled into a steady glide heading for the small bay we intended to land on, but we were coming in too high and would not make the landing area! Walter applied full power and we overshot the peninsula and had to attempt another landing. We circled the tiny peninsula and started our approach again. Walter applied one notch of flap, and aimed the aircraft towards the center of the little bay. Suddenly, the aircraft started to vibrate and shudder. It felt like something had come loose on the airframe. He attempted to return the power setting to approximately 2200 RPM, still the engine labored and backfired and the RPM dropped to 1500 without any changes in the throttle setting. This was not a good sign for a new engine!

Walter applied carb heat, changed the mixture control and still we had no control over the RPM setting! He was able to lower it to 1100 RPM, but could not increase past 1500 RPM. Suddenly, there was a bang and a crack as the engine backfired! When he tried to apply more power it backfired again, so Walter decided to land and have a good look at the engine and carburetor after we were secured at the dock. We skimmed along the surface of the water and the floats settled into the dark blue waters of the lake. While we were taxiing towards the dock the engine backfired, then backfired again, then smoke coughed up around the cowlings. We all thought the worst - that the engine was on fire. Walter shut the fuel off and waited for the vibration to stop, then got out of the aircraft and stood on the floats and paddled the plane towards the dock. We decided to unload all the gear before Walter started the engine again so we wouldn't lose everything in case there was a fire. As evening was fast approaching we decided not to look at the engine or carburetor problem as all the cowlings had to be removed first. Instead, we decided to check out the cabin, get a nice fire going, have a hot rum and coffee and discuss what could be wrong with the aircraft.

Walter and Ken having hot rum inside the cabin at Pichimi Lake

The large cook stove had a reddish glow around the area where the chimney attached to the stove and we could feel the radiant heat bouncing off our little mugs of hot rum. We placed a big cast-iron frying pan on the stove to cook our T-bone steaks. The smell of birch firewood, hot grease and searing steaks brought water to our mouths. We ate our meal, drank our rum, and soon the warm glow of the rum and the warmth of the fire had us all ready for bed. We fell asleep to the sound of mice running over the tarps and the crackle of the fire.

The next morning we rose to smell of fresh coffee perking on the stove and bacon frying in the pan. Breakfast consisted of steaks, bacon, and toast made over the open fire. The butter was like concrete as it had frozen inside the cabin during the night. We chipped flakes off it and placed it on our toast, and with a large glob of a raspberry jam we had a meal fit for a king. After the dishes were done and put away we got dressed in warm pants and boots and decided to have a look at the airplane. We had only a limited supply of tools, so whatever we were going to do we would have to do it with a screwdriver, crescent wrench, hammer and some spare nuts and bolts.

The first thing we did was to remove the upper cowlings and check the engine and carburetor for anything obvious. Nothing appeared to be out of place, and the engine was shiny and clean. We decided to run the engine up and see what happened when we increased the power setting. It started smoothly and when we increased throttle setting then it started to backfire and flames jumped out of the throat of the carburetor. We decided that the problem was not with the engine but rather with the brand new carburetor. Just to be sure it wasn't an ignition problem we switched the magnetos back and forth and increased the throttle setting, but the carburetor backfired no matter which magneto it ran on. We were concerned about the flames coming out of the carburetor, as we were scared the whole engine would catch on fire. We extinguish the fire in the carburetor with a well-placed snowball. We checked the fuel lines and looked for anything apparent on the carburetor, but everything looked all right. We decided that our major problem was with the carburetor and that we should try to have one flown in to us. We spent the rest of the day trying to figure out how we were going to notify anyone of our predicament and finally decided we would have to issue a Mayday on the radio. The weather had started to change and the drizzle changed to snow. Since no one could fly in this weather, we decided to go hunting and worry about the airplane tomorrow.

We changed into our blaze orange hunting clothes, got our rifles and ammunition, binoculars, cheesecloth in case we shot an animal and some plastic tarps to keep the snow off our shoulders and went down the lake to our hunting grounds. It was snowing very hard by now with about two inches of fresh snow on the ground, which made it very easy to track an animal, or to trail him in the event we did shoot one. We climbed into the 14- foot aluminum boat that had been left there by the previous trapper and headed towards the clearing about a mile from our camp. There was an old abandoned airstrip at the south end of the lake that had grown over with willows, an ideal place for moose to feed. We approached the sandy beach at the south end of the lake, shut the motor off and pulled the boat up on shore and walked along the beach. The sand was covered with snow and we found some tracks, which we thought were moose, but they may have been caribou.

I took a moose caller out of my backpack and made several calls, which are actually more like a grunting sound. Dennis suddenly stopped and turned around as if he had heard something, but Walter and I continued walking along the shore. We heard a grunt, then a crash in the willows that sounded like a freight train heading straight towards us. The soft snow muffled our footsteps, and the wind was blowing offshore so if it was a moose he couldn't smell us or hear us.

Suddenly, the peaceful afternoon was shattered by the sound of a rifle shot, followed by two more! Dennis was shooting at something, but we weren't sure what. We headed back towards the boat, looking for Dennis's orange hunting jacket. Soon we noticed an orange dot moving up and down in the willows. As we approached him we both hollered out, "What the hell are you shooting at?"

"I think I hit a young bull," Dennis yelled back. "He was heading your way."

A bull moose that Dennis shot in a clearing on Pichimi Lake

Soon we picked up a blood trail in the fresh snow. Now there's nothing more dangerous than a wounded moose in a thick willow patch. We decided to sit in the boat and have a cup of coffee to allow the moose to lie down. After about twenty minutes we picked up the trail and followed it for about a hundred yards. There in a small clearing was a good-sized bull moose. We approach the animal cautiously as we were not sure if it was still alive. When we had confirmed that it was dead we dressed the animal out and packed the meat in cheesecloth bags, mounted it on our backpacks and transported the bags back to the boat. We estimated that we had five to six hundred pounds of meat and about six hundred pounds of hunters in our small aluminum boat, so there wasn't much free board for our trip back to the cabin. It was starting to get dark now and we could hear wolves farther back on the airstrip. They must've picked up the scent of the fresh kill and were heading down towards the lake to clean up any of the entrails that had been left. The howling of wolves always makes the back of my hair stand up! We also knew that by morning there would be hardly any trace of the moose left.

When we finally arrived back at the cabin we took a few photographs, as everything around us resembled a pristine, winter postcard. We hung the meat in the shed attached to the cabin so we could keep it cool without it freezing. We cut off three nice steaks and a chunk of moose liver for our supper and celebrated with hot rum and coffee, boiled the moose tongue and ate it with hot mustard and pieces of bread while the smell of liver and onions filled the air! Soon the long shadows of night swept across our camp and the sky started to clear. The temperature dropped to -15°C and the brilliant blue, green, and violet of the northern lights filled the sky. Only then did we feel alone, completely alone, isolated in this beautiful part of northern Canada.

One day our cabin was warm and dry the next morning it was damp and cold and a winter wonderland

The next morning we started to work on the plane. We had left the cowlings off the engine and covered everything with a large tarp the night before. Walter suggested he try to start the engine and see if he could run the RPM up high enough for takeoff speed while Dennis and I stood behind the propeller to see if we could figure out what was wrong with the carburetor. We had to prime the engine, as the outside temperature was about -10°C. The engine started and the oil pressure and temperature rose slowly before we applied more power. Once the engine reached operating temperature, Walter applied more power. Suddenly there was a loud bang and flames shot out of the carburetor about two feet into the air. The extra fuel that had been pumped into the carburetor when we had primed the engine suddenly burst into flame. We picked up several handfuls of snow and jammed it down the throat of the carburetor. This was a pretty scary place to be as we had a whirling propeller stopping us from getting back to shore from off the dock, and flames were burning very close to the fuel lines.

Walter shut the fuel off to the engine and the flames slowly died down. When it stopped we dug the snow out of the carburetor and checked it and the engine and fuel lines for damage. Nothing was apparent but this was too dangerous and could damage the engine, so we decided to see if we could radio for help. We tried to make a radio call to Footner Lake, and then called to any aircraft that might be in the area, but we were unable to make contact with anybody. Since we were unable to contact anyone locally we decided to put out a worldwide distress call on the international frequency of 121.5. The normal procedure is to repeat Mayday three consecutive times and give your aircraft identification, plus your location if you know where you are. I went to the radio and adjusted the frequency to 121.5 and repeated "Mayday, Mayday, Mayday, this is RKO, this is Romeo, Kilo, Oscar. We have major engine problems on a Cessna 180 on floats. Our location is on the east end of Pitchimi Lake, 130 nautical miles east of Footner Lake, Alberta. Then I repeated the latitude, and longitude of our position. I repeated the distress call several times, but had no acknowledgments. We decided to try again in the morning with the engine running which would provide more power to the batteries.

An aircraft doing an aerial drop of the new carburetor into the water in a waterproof container

The next morning I awoke to the smell of fresh coffee brewing on the old cook stove. I poured a cup and added a little rum just for flavor and went outside to inhale the morning air. I was scanning the skyline for any sign of an aircraft when I noticed directly above the cabin a contrail from a jet airliner. I remembered from my flight training that commercial airlines were required to monitor 121.5, the emergency frequency, at all times. Quickly, I ran to the aircraft and without starting the engine put the master switch on, radios to on, and transmitted on 121.5, "Mayday, Mayday, Mayday, this is RKO do you copy over."

There was a crackle in the speaker and in my headset I heard, "Roger RKO. This is Northwest Orient flight 625. We copy you 5 by 5."

"Northwest Orient could you please relay our Mayday to Footner Lake air radio and Edmonton ATC and inform them RKO has a major engine problem and is stranded at Pitchimi Lake in northern Alberta." I also gave them our latitude and longitude. I heard Footner Lake answer, but because I was unable to talk to them directly Northwest Orient relayed the message for me that they would send help. Back at Footner Lake, Dave had been monitoring the air radio and had overheard our Mayday. He had replaced the engine in RKO as well as the carburetor and he thought our problem was with the carburetor. He and another pilot packaged up the old carburetor and placed it in a waterproof, container with tools and directions on how to replace it. He secured bubble pack all around it as his intent was to do an aerial drop to replace the faulty carburetor. We didn't expect any help until the next morning, but to our great surprise about at 13:00 hours we heard the sound of another aircraft. We ran to our aircraft to established radio contact with Dave. When we were able to get him he said the problem was carburetor related and that he was going to do an aerial drop into the water with our old carburetor.

We watched the aircraft fly low along the lake and the passenger side door opened, but nothing came out. He circled again and put a couple notches of flap on, slowing the aircraft right down as he flew along the shoreline. Again the passenger door opened and a green container bounced off the wheel and into the water. Dennis was already in the boat, started the engine and headed to where the container was bobbing in the water. When he returned to shore we checked out the carburetor and everything looked okay. We talked to Dave for a while before he returned to Footner Lake. He said if we required another floatplane they would have to charter one from Hay River in the Northwest Territories.

The next morning we were up early, as we wanted to try out the new carburetor. After we had placed a gas heater in the engine compartment so we would have a warm place to work we shut all fuel off, removed the fuel lines from the old carburetor and proceeded to replace it with the one Dave had dropped off. About two hours later we had the carburetor replaced, the fuel lines connected and we were ready to start the engine. We primed the engine, and then started it. It jumped to life and ran very smoothly. Walter slowly increased the throttle setting to 1500 RPM and it ran very well and did not backfire, which was a good sign. He was able to get the RPM to 1700 but no higher, and this was not enough for takeoff! We had fixed one problem, but we were unable to get to the 2600 RPM required to get us off the lake. We had told Dave that if everything went well we would climb to an altitude where we could radio Footner Lake to let him know everything was okay, but if we didn't contact him we would need an aircraft mechanic to fly in to help us with our problem.

We were unable to radio Footner Lake, so the next morning when Dave didn't hear from us he requested a floatplane from Hay River to meet Hank, Dave's partner, at Margaret Lake where there was a small strip next to the floatplane dock. Hank flew a Cessna 150 out to Margaret Lake and there he met up with a charter pilot from Hay River and together they headed for Pitchimi Lake.

Our mechanic Hank Paul's arriving in a chartered float plane from Hay River Northwest Territories

We had just finished breakfast when we heard the sound of a small aircraft in the distance. We scanned the horizon and suddenly saw the outline of a floatplane. We weren't sure if this was help for us, or just a bunch of hunters heading for Wood Buffalo National Park, but it was a relief to see another floatplane in the area! We radioed the aircraft, and sure enough it was Hank coming to help us with our engine problem.

After they had landed Hank went over to our aircraft, started the engine and attempted to get it up to flying RPM. He was unsuccessful so he immediately shut the engine off and began a physical inspection of the carburetor and all the fuel lines. After a time he said, "What's this?"

We all exclaimed together, "What's what?"

Hank took a screwdriver and pointed to the side of the intake manifold. We looked at the engine, and still could not see any visible problems. "Right here," he said. We looked again and we still saw nothing. But on closer inspection we noticed a small gap between the rubber connector on the intake manifold and the side of the engine. Hank explained. "When the carburetor backfired it blew the rubber connecting tubes off the connection to the intake manifold to the engine, allowing air to be sucked into the engine rather than fuel. Apparently the C clamps were not secured properly when the engine was assembled."

Hank connected all the tubes and replaced the C clamps, attached all the fuel lines and we were ready to try the engine again. He primed the engine, turned on the ignition switch, pressed the starter and the engine sprang to life. He slowly increased the throttle setting, to 1500 RPM, then to 2000, and finally to 2600. We had now enough RPM for takeoff. Our problem was solved and we gratefully thanked Hank and the other pilot for coming to our assistance. Then we loaded some of our gear and the moose meat into his aircraft, as this would reduce our weight for takeoff as we had decided to follow them home in case we had any more trouble.

We broke camp, put out the fire in the stove and made sure the cabin was just as we had found it. Hank and the other pilot taxied out first and waited for us in the little bay until we were airborne. It was one of those beautiful fall afternoons and we were reluctant to go home, but for the sake of safety it was better to leave now and have the aircraft thoroughly checked out. Well, another non-eventful trip. And this was my first real Mayday!

RKO back in the air again after engine repair

Chapter 13

October 31, 1976 was Halloween night when ghosts and goblins start to roam. Our girls, Donna and Bobbie, were set to go trick-or-treating and Helen and I were going to spend the evening at home to greet the kids who were making the rounds in our rural area. The wind started to blow around 11:00 p.m. and continued through the night. When we awoke the next morning our garbage can was turned over and most of the rubbish was scattered around the yard. I went outside to clean it up, not sure if the wind or trick-or-treaters had caused the damage.

Bad day at Bear Lake Alberta CF-HDN on its back

The next morning was going to be busy for me, as I had arranged to do a changeover on my aircraft, planning to remove the floats and put wheels on the plane for winter. The crane I had hired to lift the aircraft was scheduled for 12:00 p.m. About ten people from work had said they would come to help steady the aircraft while we lifted it into the air so the floats could be removed. About 9:00 a.m. I loaded the wheels and gear legs, tools, etc. into the truck and headed for Bear Lake where I kept my aircraft on the beach, as it was nice and sandy and easy on the bottom of the floats.

The plan was to remove the floats, install the wheels, and then taxi down the beach road to the highway having first removed the highway signs along the side of the road so that the wings wouldn't hit them on takeoff. As in previous years, I sent two vehicles to block traffic each way while I was taking off. I thought it might be against the law to use a secondary highway as a runway, but I never asked and nobody ever told me, and the road was much better than most runways I had landed on.

When I got to the beach I couldn't believe my eyes. There was my aircraft turned upside down, with the tail driven deep into the sand! My heart stopped for a moment as I tried to figure out what could have happened. It was completely upside down, floats in the air with the propeller buried in the sand. What could have happened? It had been Halloween, but I didn't think vandals could do anything like this. What was I to do? I had no insurance on the airframe, so any damages would have to be paid out of my own pocket. Had it been the wind that had perhaps lifted the aircraft and dropped it upside down on the sand? It would have made a lot more sense if I had been flying and slid into the beach and then flipped over, but to this day I have no idea what flipped the plane over.

Remembering the unusually high winds from the night before, I could only think that perhaps a small tornado had picked the aircraft up and dropped it on the sand about ten feet away from where I had parked it. We can add this to the list of the many unsolved mysteries about flying. But what to do? How to turn the aircraft over? We needed to do this without causing any more damage to the airframe. By now the people who were going to help with the aircraft had arrived and they were as incredulous as I at what they saw.

We decided to remove the propeller so as not to cause any strain on the crankshaft of the engine. Then I went around and inspected the airframe and made a list of the damage. The tail feathers were bent and ruffled and the wings had several dents along the leading edge but the flaps and aileron seemed undamaged. I couldn't see how much damage was done to the cockpit until we got the aircraft turned over. The floats seemed all right but it was very difficult to check them out until they were in the water. The main part of the fuselage seemed undamaged. I estimated in my head that a year's salary would just about pay for the repairs.

The Crew and the Crane required to turn the aircraft over

The gang from work and the Crane required two turn over the aircraft

I decided to call Dave Cathcart at Liberty Air in Footner Lake, who had been my aircraft mechanic and mentor since 1972. If anybody had an answer, Dave would be the man. I told him what had happened. He couldn't believe it. How do you pick up a 2500-pound floatplane and turn it on its back? I related to him what damage had been done but I couldn't see the underside of the aircraft. He said the first thing to do was to remove the propeller, then dig under the wings and place some foam rubber, or any other type of padding we could find, between the sand and the leading edge. Then we should attach a rope to the tail of the plane and pull slowly so that the aircraft could pivot on its nose and the tips of each float.

We attached a rope to the tail and then to the trailer hitch on my truck, then placed several ropes around the wings and the tail so that we could steady the aircraft when it got in the air. To make sure there wasn't any more damage done when the plane started to pivot, I had my friend Dennis drive the truck so I could be near the plane during the operation. As the truck moved slowly forward the aircraft moved upward, finally standing on its nose where the propeller had been removed and balancing on the tips of the two floats.

Now we had to bring it back down without doing any damage to the bottom of the floats. We untied the rope to the trailer hitch, slowly allowing the aircraft to ease forward while maintaining tension on the rope till the plane was sitting safely on its floats.

I don't think we did any more damage to the airframe, but we scratched a little paint and bent one wing tip. Now I had a chance to assess how much damage had been done to the cockpit. I thought the windscreen would be cracked, but it wasn't. There was little or no damage to the top of the aircraft. Now what could lift an aircraft completely into the air, turn it over, lay it down on the sand, and not even break the Plexiglas in the windscreen? I just don't know. Maybe the same aliens that makes crop circles!

Dave said the wings should be removed and the fuel tanks drained and disconnected, which we did. However, we needed a trailer large enough to carry the main part of the fuselage with the floats, and the wings and the struts had to be packaged up so as not to damage them further. We decided to remove the wings while the aircraft was still on the sand to make it easier to remove the bolts and wing struts.

Down but not out badly bent tail and wings October 31, 1976

When we had the wings removed we carried them up to a grassy area not far from the beach. I had arranged to get a crane from the local power company, used to lift and set large poles. When the crew arrived with the crane we had to tell the story all over again. Meanwhile, Dennis had gone to get a flatbed trailer. When he arrived back we decided to lift the aircraft onto the trailer and pad and secure the wings on each side of the floats. The trailer was small enough that I could pull it with my four-wheel drive truck but the load was too high, too wide, and the funniest thing ever seen on a trailer. We walked over to the telephone at the local campground and called Dave at Liberty Airways. Dave told us to bring the airplane to High Level where he lived. Dennis and I decided we would leave the next night, as it was a Sunday if we left late enough there would be little or no traffic on the road. We had about five hundred miles to trans-port the plane. Dennis and I headed out about 4:00 p.m. Sunday evening, expecting we would get to High Level about 8:00 a.m. Monday morning. So off we went down the Bear Lake Road till we got to Fox Creek, then turned north. We took turns driving as we figured it would take eight to ten hours to get there. Most cars and all of the big trucks stayed far to the right as they approached us, probably thinking the airplane was going to land on the highway. We passed Peace River and were heading for Manning when we saw flashing red and blue lights in the rear view mirror.

A policeman pulled us over and directed us to the next truck stop where he said he would meet us. When we got there we went into a coffee shop and had breakfast. The policeman arrived with a tape measure, notepad, and a book of tickets. That's traffic tickets he hadn't used yet! He said, "You're too wide, you're too high, and you have no lights on the wing struts. What do you guys think you are doing?" And I told him in the nicest way possible the story of the aircraft mystery. I don't think he believed that either! He said we definitely had to do something about being too wide. He suggested we buy four flashlights, place two facing forward, and two facing towards the rear. He gave us a piece of red flagging material to place over the lens of the flashlights facing towards the rear. But we didn't get a ticket! We taped the flashlights in place and we were soon on the road again. I also turned on the navigational lights on the aircraft. Now it did look like this airplane was going to land on the highway! So, dumb and dumber, headed towards High Level.

We arrived at Footner Lake airport about 10 o'clock in the morning, just in time for coffee! Dave started to laugh as we pulled up to the hanger, and he didn't stop till I had finished my first cup of coffee. I related the story all over again, and it still didn't make any sense!

Once inside the hanger we removed the wings from the trailer, attached the aircraft to the overhead crane, pulled the trailer out and rested it on the hanger floor. Dave did a quick assessment of the damage, but he couldn't make a final decision until the wings and tail sections were completely apart. So Dennis and I decided to get a couple hours of shuteye before heading home. Our trip home was quiet and basically uneventful, which was a pleasant change!

Several times during the winter some of the pilots in the Edson flying club ferried me to High Level so I could check on the progress of the work on my aircraft. By February 13, 1977 it was completely repaired - the date I flew back home to Edson.

The aircraft completely repaired and back in the water on Pichimi Lake Alberta 1977

CHAPTER 14

Not all my flights were hair-raising adventures. Some were just normal everyday picnics, overnight camping and spending time in the wilderness which was always more fun when shared with friends and family.

The following is a recollection of one such story. The date was May 25, 1973 when we, Bill and Sylvia McAllister, their baby Rob, and Dave Cathcart, the owner of Liberty Airways who also flew in on that weekend, and also Helen and I set off for Thurston Lake for a few days of fishing and camping. The latter part of May and the first part of June are usually the best times for fishing in the north. Most of the ice was off the lake and the mosquitoes and black flies were bad, but not too bad. The following is Bill's recollection of our weekend some 30 years ago:

"I'm not sure if we went to Thurston Lake with Dave Cathcart or if Ken flew us in, but I do know that I had flown with Dave once before. Anyhow, Thurston Lake was quite an experience for me. Our son, Rob, was seven months old so we brought his car bed and high chair amongst other things. I probably had enough clothes for him to stay at Thurston another month. During the day, Ken and Bill made a very smoky fire in a barrel so that the many mosquitoes would not eat us alive. Rob sat by the fire in his high chair with netting over him and seemed quite content. He slept through the night and in the morning we warmed up his milk bottle in our sleeping bag.

Ken and Bill went fishing in an old boat that was pulled up on shore. Bill caught a twenty-six pound fish that was jumping around in the boat and Ken was trying to hit it with an oar. Helen and I thought it was quite funny. Later when we were fishing Ken hooked a fish and the first time it came by the boat it looked like a pickerel, then there was a splash around the end of the line and the next time it came around it was a northern pike. (In the north the northern pike is called a Jack fish, and the walleye is called a pickerel.) When we got the fish into the boat it was a pickerel with marks behind the gills where the Jack fish had gotten a hold on it. We also caught a twenty pound Jack, which we brought back with us."

The following is Sylvia's recollection of that weekend: "On Saturday night there was a rainstorm and that's when Bill developed a fever. We feared that he would be stranded there but the next day the sun was shining and he felt well again. One of my favorite recollections of the trip was to have had fresh fish for breakfast. It was so yummy, the best breakfast I've ever had. Also, I saw how a fish heart still beats when you hold it in your hand after it has been killed. On the way home, Rob slept on the floor in the back of the plane. Ken asked me if I could see an island below us, and when I said, "no" then he took the plane down at a very fast clip. Needless to say, my heart was in my mouth and I never did see the island. But Helen had a chuckle out of that one. Anyhow, everyone including Rob had a fun weekend."

On another such adventure Helen and I and our two girls, Roberta and Donna, and our good friend Alex Patterson planned to go to Caribou Lake for a weekend of fishing and camping. On July 13, 1973 Alex and I took off from Footner Lake and flew in with the tent, food, and fishing gear. Then I came back and picked up Helen and the two girls. I always took the back seat out of the airplane on such occasions so I could load more gear. This meant the girls had no seat belts. They would lean against the front seats and chatter in my ear, "Let's do the roller coaster dad." I would quickly drop the nose of the aircraft, creating a negative gravity situation, which allowed the girls the float around in the back of the aircraft. To them this was like being on a roller coaster, or better still flying to the moon with zero gravity. They just loved this part of flying!

Our camp at Caribou Lake

When we arrived at Caribou Lake, Alex had the tents up, a fire on, and the cast iron frying pan on the stove full of pork and beans. The girls liked to make pork and beans sandwiches, which meant there were more beans on their faces and clothes, than between the two pieces of bread. A whiskey jack soon made a short order of anything that fell on the ground. Our first day there the weather was great and the fishing was wonderful. There is something very soothing about sitting around a campfire telling ghost stories and toasting marshmallows over an open fire.

The next day our world changed. The wind got up and it started to rain, confining us to our tents. The rain made a pleasant sound against the tight canvas. We zippered our sleeping bags together and with out feet covered and warm we played Snap, and Hearts to pass the time away and waited for the weather to clear. Suddenly, the tent began shaking and the center pole started waving back and forth as the tent pegs loosened around the edges of the tent. Before long the only thing holding the tent up was the center pole.

Alex and I crawled outside to see if we could do anything to secure the tent. We were able to place four large rocks on each corner but this wasn't going to last long. Alex's tent was already down so we placed a large rock in the center of it so it wouldn't blow away. Helen and the girls held the center pole, while Alex and I placed tent pegs through the loops and into the sand. They didn't hold, and by now we were all soaking wet. The wind was blowing much stronger, and we couldn't hold the tents up. This campsite had a forestry fuel shed on it, called fuel cache number 75. It was a metal shed used to store aviation fuel for helicopters and airplanes in the event of a forest fire. I had a key on my key ring that we used to gain access to forestry roads. To fix their radios and transmitter sites. I thought perhaps the same make of lock would be used on the sheds as was used on their gates. I tried my key in the large padlock and twisted it back-and-forth and finally the padlock popped open. I opened the door but the wind caught it, throwing me to the ground. I got up and jammed a log against the door to keep it open while I went to get Helen and the girls. I held the center pole up while she gathered all our belongings and headed for the shed. Alex's gear and sleeping bag were soaking wet so we left them in the tent and placed another rock on them. I re-checked the aircraft to make sure it was secure and headed into the wind. We were cold and wet, but we had shelter from the storm. We would have liked to light our gas stove, but because of the large storage of fuel in the shed we felt this was not a good idea. However, we found a supply of metallic sleeping bags, some previously used and some brand new, used by firefighters.

We wrapped them around us and soon we were warm, a little damp, but warm. We had a thermos of hot chocolate left over from breakfast so we ate chocolate chip cookies, drank hot chocolate, and soon we were warm on the inside as well as on the outside.

After the storm let up a bit, Alec and I started to rummage around the shed to see what we could find. We found an old potbelly stove used to heat the firefighters' tents and about six feet of stovepipe. We decided to set up the stove outside, but in the doorway so that the heat would radiate inside the shed, using the firewood we had cut previously that was stored outside under a tarp. We set up the stove, placed chunks of dried tamarack and birch bark into it, added a little liquid fire [aviation fuel] into the belly, threw in a match and swoosh we had a fire. Soon the belly of the stove and the stovepipe were cherry red, filling the shed with radiant heat.

We cooked supper on the stove and brewed some coffee and made hot chocolate. Our sleeping bags were still damp so we laid them over some of the fuel drums to dry. We snuggled down into our space-age sleeping bags, which looked like large sheets of tinfoil with some type of material attached on one side. They were very light and very warm and they reflected the heat towards our bodies. During the night we closed the door to keep the wind out, as well as other such beasties that might be wandering around.

The eaves were open to provide ventilation for the fuel drums. Towards dusk the birds had found a roosting place in the open eaves, but they didn't bother us, they just fluffed their feathers up and went to sleep. Soon we heard the pitter patter of little feet on our tinfoil covering. I wasn't sure what it was, but I didn't really want to know as I thought it might be mice, maybe even squirrels, but I fervently hoped it wasn't rats. Everyone was sound asleep when I turned my small flashlight on and found a furry little mouse sitting on my chest. I didn't want to say anything to alarm anybody or we would have been awake all night long.

The next morning came and it was still raining. The sky was overcast with a very low ceiling. When I went outside, I couldn't see the top of the surrounding hills. This meant that there would be no flying today, at least not until I could get over the hills. The weather started to clear about 8:00 p.m. that evening, but we decided to stay one more night and go home the next morning. Fortunately, most of our gear and sleeping bags had dried out by this time. The fishing was excellent so we had fresh pickerel fried in butter. It doesn't get any better than this.

The weather here can change so fast. We woke up the next morning to white, puffy, cumulus clouds. With the aroma of freshly perked coffee in the air and a slight northerly breeze to keep the mosquitoes and black flies down we were truly content although we were all scratching our heads. We had been attacked by black flies during the night. I checked Donnas' neck and underneath her hairline to see if she got into some ticks, or had black fly bites. But what I found was much more disturbing - lice, body lice. We must have picked them up from the sleeping bags. We checked Bobbie and found the same thing, except she had long hair and there were better places to hide. We stripped the girls down and got them into the lake and scrubbed them and their hair with dishwashing soap. We burnt their clothes and underwear and dressed them in clean garments from their backpacks.

We followed the kids into the lake, bathed and washed our hair then put on clean clothes. We shook out our sleeping bags and laid them out in the sun then packed them securely in green garbage bags. I certainly didn't want to burn my Arctic Three Star sleeping bag, nor did I want lice in my aircraft.

We arrived home on July 16, 1973. Alex and I sprayed the sleeping bags with bug spray then resealed them and stored them in the hanger for a couple weeks. When we got the girls home they were put in the bathtub and scrubbed and polished till their mother was sure there were no more bugs!

This next story is about flying trappers into remote regions of the north so that they could pursue their craft, a distinct way of life. This trip started on September 11, 1971 flying from Wekusko Lake, about ten nautical miles east of Snow Lake. Ernie Stoltz, a local trapper from the area, had asked me to fly him into Roberts Lake. He wanted to get ready for his fall trapping season. I had never been into Roberts Lake, nor could I find it on my flight maps. So I totally relied on Ernie to navigate me there.

We loaded his burlap bags of traps, stretching boards, boxes of food and flour into the aircraft. The last thing we loaded was Ernie's rifle and shotgun. Once we were airborne, with the windows and doors were tightly closed the fragrance of the traps, stretching boards and fleshing boards permeated the air. The beaver fat on Ernie's pants wasn't rancid or foul, and the pungent odor of beaver castors that emanated from his plaid shirt set the mood for this trip. This fragrance is not obnoxious, but very soothing and pleasant and represents a lifestyle almost gone in the north. When a man, his rifle and his love for the wilderness and the animals that live there are related to you by song, storytelling, or just by silence, it makes you feel you never want to return to civilization again.

Ernie guided me along Crow Duck Bay, over some marshland, and past an abandoned mineshaft to a small lake. "This is it," he said. "There should be a small cabin and a dock at the far end." And there it was just as he had said. I circled the lake a couple of times to check for snags and stumps and everything looked okay. I landed and pulled up to the rickety old dock. Planks were missing so I had to be careful trying to get to the shore. We unloaded the rifles first and Ernie loaded the shotgun and circled the cabin to check for bears. I unloaded the rest of the gear while Ernie opened the cabin. Bears had left the cabin alone, but not the mice and squirrels. Anything that had been made out of plastic or cardboard had been chewed. The first traps that he set were to catch some of these little varmints.

Ernie started a fire and put on some water for tea. He wiped out the cast-iron frying pan, put some grease in it and placed it on the fire. He went down to the lake and fetched a pail of water and scooped some water into a bowl. Then he added some flour, baking powder and lots of raisins and mixed all the ingredients together. Soon he had a little ball of dough with raisins sticking out all over. He rolled it out and cut it into two equal pieces, then placed it in the hot frying pan. Soon we were eating the traditional native bread known as bannock. The musty smell of the cabin had now been transformed into that of a bakery. I enjoyed the bannock, covered with marmalade washed down with tea.

I flew home the same day and never saw or heard of Ernie Stoltz again. Maybe he is still in the bush. He probably got out after the lake froze when he could get out by skidoo.

Chapter 15

It was in the fall of 1974 when Ken and Jill Munro received word that they were being transferred from High Level, Alberta to Brooks, Alberta. At the same time Helen and I received notice that we were being transferred to Edson, Alberta. After the news had sunk in we had to inform our children that they would be leaving the north and their friends and relocating to a new town. We felt a little sad, as we had lived in that part of northern Canada since 1967. We weren't sure we would ever get a chance to return north again or if there were good lakes in this new location to dock a floatplane. One thing I did know for sure, the second passion in life, skiing, would be fulfilled as we would be close to Jasper and have access to the Rocky Mountains.

Now that we knew we were going to leave the north we decided to have a joint going away party, and Thurston Lake would be an ideal location as Ken could land his aircraft, which was on wheels, on the small grass strip adjacent to the lake. I could fly my floatplane and land on the lake so we could have the best of both worlds. The location of this lake is very close to the 60th parallel where the northern part of the provinces end and the Northwest Territories start. If you live and play around the 60th parallel you leave your heart there. I know this to be true as I have traveled all over Canada and many parts of the world and the place that has brought me the most happiness and peace of mind is northern Canada.

High Level, Alberta where we were living was a transient town. People had come here to develop the oil and gas industry, and I had been sent north to provide communication

Ken and Jill and their newfound home at Thurston Lake Alberta
this was her going away party from High Level

to the oil companies so they could communicate with their head offices in Calgary and other parts of the world. With exploration comes many non-permanent residents - people sent here for a short period of time that are just passing through and nothing seems permanent. While we were here we had subsidized housing and a northern allowance, but all this would be lost when we moved south.

On one late August morning we set out for our going away party. Included in "The Last Supper" were: Roger Dotzler, Tom Ingledew, Jim Knox, Roger Overholt, Ken and Jill Munro, and Helen and I. What a crew! On the previous Thursday I had flown all the guys into the beach on Thurston to set up camp. This was a good location as it had a creek a nice sandy beach where I could secure the floatplane. Early that morning Ken had to fly to Brooks in his company's super

Cub aircraft. He was to return later that afternoon and fly Helen and Jill into Thurston Lake in his own aircraft, then I was to meet them and ferry them across to the other side to our campsite. It was better to taxi across the lake rather than fly as darkness had set in.

Once the camp was set up and a large bonfire was lighting up the evening sky with sparks and dancing flames I flew back to the other side of the lake. I healed the floatplane up on a log and waited. The sound of laughter echoed across the lake as the boys danced and drank around the campfire. The long daylight hours in the north were gone and darkness and the northern lights were back. It was getting late and it seemed Ken should be here by now. If he didn't come soon the landing strip would be cloaked in darkness and he would be unable to land. I decided to turn on my aircraft radio tuned into 126.7 to see if he was in radio range. As I was doing this I thought I heard an aircraft and I scanned the southern skies for a dot or flashing beacon, but I saw nothing. I transmitted out on my radio Ken's aircraft identification. My headset crackled then I heard, "I'm coming."

I replied, "Who's coming?"

He replied. "Mackenzie coming." I knew it was Ken when he started to laugh.

First I saw the flashing red beacon, then the outline of the wings and fuselage. The aircraft, silhouetted against the northern lights that were dancing with purple, green and blue hues, looked like it had come from another planet. Ken didn't waste any time landing as the strip was already covered with evening mist. He left his landing lights on as he taxied down the narrow path towards my aircraft. Most of their gear had been flown in during the afternoon so all I had to do was transport four people.

Helen and Jill sat in the back with Ken and me in the front. Ken pushed us away from the shore and I started the engine and headed towards the campfire on the far side of the lake. The campfire was our navigational beacon, as we had no other way to locate the distant shore. It was now dark, very dark, and the windscreen began to fog over because of our breathing. I opened my window to allow the air to circulate and keep the windscreen clear. After a few minutes, I could barely see the fire on the distant shore and I thought I might be going in the wrong direction. I decided to flash my landing lights and turn on my rotary beacon as it could be seen for up to five miles. For a moment I saw sparks heading into the air, then nothing. There was no shoreline, absolutely nothing, just blackness and a red glow from the instrument panel. I revved the engine up and, flashed the landing lights, trying to get the attention of the guys on the opposite shore, but this didn't seem to be working. We thought they should be able to hear the aircraft coming as sound carries so clearly across water.

The boys that were supposed to keep the fire lit! The next morning it was cold and wet

I decided to shut the aircraft off and have Ken stand on the floats and holler as loudly as he could to attract their attention. Ken opened the door and stepped out on the floats just as the engine was winding down, but there was still enough thrust to keep the plane moving forward. The instant Ken stood on the float and started to call out to the guys on the shore I knew something was wrong. The attitude of the aircraft was changing - the nose of the aircraft was starting to point skyward and soon all I could see out of the windscreen were stars and the northern lights.

Ken, realizing something was wrong also, moved forward on the floats towards the propeller. The girls, who had been busy talking, stopped chatting and Helen asked,

"What's up?"

I replied, "We're trying to contact the boys on the shore to keep the fire going." Suddenly, there was a response from the far shore. It looked like someone had poured gasoline on the fire and the flames formed a mushroom cloud going almost sixty feet into the air. This was great. We now had the shoreline in sight.

Ken started to work his way back along the float till he reached the door, but the aircraft took on a very tail-heavy attitude. When he moved back to the front of the float this helped level out the aircraft. I thought the extra weight with the girls in the back seat might be contributing to the problem so I asked them lean over Ken's seat to put the center of gravity further forward. This worked, and the plane leveled out. Ken started to move to the rear again while the girls still bent over his seat. The nose of the aircraft started to move up, causing the tail to sink into the water. I yelled to Ken to get back, and we leveled off again.

Something was wrong, very wrong. Then Ken said, "Maybe the rear compartments on the floats are flooded." This couldn't be as the inspection plate had a sealed o-ring, but it seemed to be the most logical answer. We discussed what to do next and decided I would start the engine, apply some throttle and that would pull the nose down thus moving the center of gravity forward. The only problem with this was that Ken had to remain outside the aircraft until the engine had started and we were moving.

Each float had a red line painted across the top as a warning not to pass or you would be too close to the propeller. Heedless of this, Ken placed one foot on the red line and the other near the spreader bar. He held onto the wing strut and yelled, "Start her up." I turned the master switch on and the magneto switch to both and reached for the starter. The UGH UGH UGH that I heard was an indication that the battery didn't have enough power to start the engine. Ken said, "Maybe if I pull down on the propeller it will help the starter." This was probably the best idea, but a very dangerous one.

When all the switches were turned off, Ken moved one foot past the red line, carefully placed the other one beside it, and grabbed the wing strut with his left hand and the propeller with his right. He slowly rotated the blade till it reached the compression point and said, "I'm ready."

I turned the master and magneto switches to on and reached for the starter. "On the count off three," I said. He replied that was okay. "One, two, three." I pulled the starter and at the same time he pulled down on the propeller. One cylinder fired, then another. The engine was running! Ken moved back on his perch to be close to the wing strut, turning towards the rear to protect him from the prop wash.

The fire on the shore had reached almost a forest fire magnitude; it probably could have been seen for fifty miles. Since we were only about a mile away Ken decided to stay on the outside of the aircraft until we reached the other side. The girls didn't seem to be worried as they continued to lean forward over the seats to provide the weight shift required to keep the nose down and the tail up. The flames grew brighter and soon we could see four men dancing around the fire and placing huge dry logs on it as sparks flew toward the stars.

I started to reduce the throttle but each time I did the plane started to sink down tail first. This meant I must approach the shore with power on, but I didn't want to knock Ken forward when I hit the sand, nor did I want to damage my prop. When I hit the shore Ken slid off the floats into the water. I shut down the engine but when it stopped the floats and the tail sank into the water. However, we were all safe, a little wet but safe. We immediately unloaded the girls and the gear to lighten the plane. The next task was to get the water out of the rear compartments. It wasn't safe to leave the plane in the water in case a storm came up and smashed the pontoons.

We set up our Coleman lanterns and hung them on some over hanging bows. First we cut some four-inch poplar trees long enough to reach under the front of the floats. These were to act as rollers so we could get the rear portion of the floats out of the water and pump them out. When we had ten to twelve logs cut we attached a rope to the front Ballard on the floats and started to pull. Helen and Jill placed the logs one by one under the keel section of the pontoons. Soon the aircraft was up on our man-made ramp. Sure enough, the rear compartments were flooded in both floats. A faulty o-ring on the inspection plate had caused this, not because we were "slightly over loaded." After the floats were pumped dry we pushed the aircraft off the ramp, turned it around and healed it up on the shore for the night. I decided to look at the battery problem in the morning when we could see more clearly.

Ken began to set up their sleeping quarters. It consisted of one tarp on the ground, sleeping bags in the middle, and another tarp on the top. Helen and I decided to sleep in our tent. As evening progressed and we were mixing orange crystals with lake water and rum or vodka, old campfire songs started to echo around the shores of the lake, joined by the odd loon call and even a lone wolf joined in the chorus.

When we awoke the next morning our mixing containers were two thirds orange colored sand mixed with the odd piece of clamshell. Perhaps when we were scooping the water for our mix we went to deep. Ken and Jill had slept under the stars but during the night it had rained and the water had run through the tarps soaking the sleeping bags, but they had had enough to drink that it didn't seem to matter to either of them.

After a wonderful breakfast of fish fried in bacon fat we were ready to check out the aircraft charging system, but first we hung Ken's and Jill's sleeping bags over some small spruce trees to dry. We checked the battery in the airplane with a voltmeter that I carried in my toolkit and found I was well below the twelve volts required to start the aircraft.

We took the battery out and transported it across the lake where we could charge it in Ken's aircraft, leaving the rest of the group behind to clean up camp and do some fishing in the creek. We knew my battery was good as it was brand new. It only required charging. When we got to Ken's plane we decided to exchange batteries. I took Ken's fully charged battery back to my plane as it is a lot easier to hand crank using the propeller to start an aircraft on land than on water. When I returned we hand cranked his engine to charge my battery. When we replaced the batteries and gave the prop a hearty twist, the engine sprang to life. After checking Ken's charging system, it indicated the battery was taking a full charge. After we had let the engine run for about twenty minutes till we thought it had charged enough, we loaded the fully charged battery into the boat and headed back across the lake to my plane. Now we both had fully charged batteries to get us home.

The hardest part about camping in the wilderness is to find a place to go "potty." We found a great place not far from camp - but far enough if you know what I mean.

The next morning I awoke to find Helen gone, but the smell of fresh coffee and of dry tamarack burning in the cook stove drifted in and out of the tent. Helen had set off for her morning constitutional on our famous commode. I decided to crawl along the beach and sneak up on her while she sat on her perch. I went along the beach, and then decided to head toward the bush where I thought she and the commode were. As I slowly crawled toward the area, the wind indicated I was in the right spot. I peered through a clump of grass and there was Helen sitting on the throne. Not twenty feet behind her stood the largest pearl gray wolf I had ever seen. It was obvious he hadn't seen her or had her scent, and she wasn't aware of him. I called out "Helen, there's the biggest wolf I have ever seen right behind you."

She screamed back at me, "Oh sure, you just want to scare me." The screech of her voice caused the wolf to dig in his four paws and get the hell out of there.

She still didn't believe me till I showed her the wolf's prints in the sand, which I'm sure measured six inches across. This was the standing joke around camp for the rest of the weekend. And nobody went to the bathroom without making as much noise as possible.

Because of my faulty charging system, everything had to be transported across the lake by boat to Ken's aircraft.

He had to make several trips in his plane to get everyone and their gear back home. Helen and Jill went out with Ken and I took Roger Dotzler with our gear out on August 18, 1974. This was a wonderful way to say good-bye to some of our friends in the north, some of whom we have never seen again. Some like Ken and Jill are still life-long friends. They presently live in Priddis, Alberta.

Chapter 16

Another adventurer began on June 25, 1976. Like most pilots talking about trips, they are usually planning more trips. This one started with Rich Sawatsky, from Grande Cache, wanting to do a long cross-country flight north. We decided to get a group together and fly from Edson to Footner Lake, then transfer to floatplanes and fly into Caribou Lake that is located east of High-Level Alberta. This was the best time of year to get a good catch of pickerel, as the ice would have just gone out of the lake. The group that went was: Myles Schnee and Dennis Lindsay from Edson; Rich, who would pilot his own plane, called a Maule Rocket. Walter Penko from High Level was to fly the second floatplane, CF RKO, into Caribou Lake; and I was to take my floatplane from Bear Lake to Footner Lake. The plan was that we would all meet up at Footner Lake.

I took Myles with me from Bear Lake, and Rich flew to Edson on wheels to pick up Dennis, then on to Footner Lake where we would all meet up and rendezvous with Walter. We landed at Footner Lake about two hours apart. After we met Walter we refueled his Cessna 180 and my Cessna 170 B, and we were ready to go. As soon as Rich landed at the airport and we had his aircraft secured, we transferred the gear to Walter's and my floatplanes.

The flight into Caribou Lake was great as we had two floatplanes, which meant everything we required could be carried in with one trip and we didn't have to ferry people or gear from Footner Lake to Caribou.

There was a fourteen-foot aluminum boat at Caribou Lake that we were allowed to use. I am not sure who actually owned it, if it had been flown in during a forest fire or if it had been brought in during the winter by skidoo by one of the trappers. After we arrived we set up camp then decided three of us would go out in the boat, and the other three could go later. This meant there were six people on this trip, but no one can remember who the sixth person was. We have checked logbooks and photos but this elusive fishing partner seems to have been a ghost.

A campfire is always special, sitting on logs around the dancing flames and telling stories of fishing trips, hunting trips, and watching as the flames light up each storyteller's face with a reddish-orange glow. The smells are something you never forget, like the aroma of pine scented pitch on logs crackling in the fire, the fragrance of aviation fuel wafting from under the cowlings of the aircraft. The smell of coffee with its deep Arabic scent, plus a dash of dark rum, adds to the perfect atmosphere for a feeling of being in paradise, perhaps even heaven on earth.

We fished very hard, but the fish weren't biting and my fishing stories were starting to lose credibility. After a full day of fishing we had caught only twenty-two fish, six we ate for supper. About nine o'clock in the evening Walter, Dennis and I decided to go out fishing and give the lake another try, leaving the rest to sit around the fire and drink rum. We motored to a spot where we had caught a few fish in the morning and cast out our lines. On the first cast we each had a fish on. Wow this was great! The hype and hollering from the boat made the guys on shore think we were just fooling around and probably weren't catching anything. About midnight we pulled the boat up on shore and counted our catch. We had caught ninety-six fish in just a couple of hours! We set up an assembly line to fillet them, with me removing the flesh from the bones and the others removing the skin and packing the fish in ice in the coolers we had brought along.

The weekend over, we broke camp and headed back to Footner Lake where we refueled my aircraft and transferred the fish and the gear to Rich's Maule rocket. Myles and I headed off earlier as Rich's plane could fly faster than my aircraft and it was a four-hour flight back to Bear Lake.

As we were approaching the town of Fox Creek, the weather started to deteriorate and low clouds and rain forced us to descend to a lower altitude. The top layer of cloud kept getting lower and lower, and when smokestacks from the gas plants south of Fox Creek were higher than my aircraft, I decided to turn around and look for another lake to land on. There were several lakes around Fox Creek, but I wasn't sure of my exact location.

The ground was partly obscured with low clouds and fog and the rain had turned to drizzle. Myles suddenly said, "There's a lake." I could see it so I turned to starboard to get a better view. I saw a dock and some fishing boats and the lake looked long enough to land and take off on. I set one notch of flaps, slipped through the mist and slid along the lake surface. I had no idea what lake this was, but according to the sign on the dock it was Smoke Lake, and which, according to our map, was just south of Fox Creek.

We secured the aircraft to the dock, and when I checked the fuel in the aircraft I decided we didn't have enough to get to Bear Lake. Since I had two empty 5-gallon fuel containers in the plane, I went over to some people camping nearby to see if they had any spare fuel. They had fuel for their outboard motors, but it was mixed with oil.

Myles decided he would hike to town to get some fuel while I cleaned up the aircraft and tried to phone home and also notify Edmonton air traffic control of our situation so they wouldn't alert air search and rescue that we were overdue on our flight plan. When Myles arrived back about two hours later we refueled the plane, and by then the overcast skies had cleared. When we finally arrived back at Bear Lake we were only six hours later than we had anticipated.

All in all, just another great fishing trip in the great outdoors.

Chapter 17

On October 6, 1981 my friend Myles and I decided to combine some fishing and hunting in the Pine Creek area, fifty miles north of Edson. It was one of those hot fall days when we arrived in Myles' 4-wheel drive at a remote area along Pine Creek, so we thought we would go for a swim after we had set up camp. We stripped down to our birthday suits and dove into a deep green pool. The water wasn't cold, it was bloody well freezing. I wondered when the water hit my private parts if I was male or female. We didn't stay in long and, refreshed, we dripped-dried in the sun.

After lunch we changed into our hunting gear and wandered up the creek to see if we could see any sign of moose or elk. About a mile upstream we saw some fresh tracks in the muddy shoreline. One was that of a large moose and the other of a grizzly, not a black bear, as we recognized tracks from the long claw marks. While being in the vicinity of a bear doesn't bother me, but a grizzly is a whole different story. Myles and I both chambered a cartridge just in case we met our furry friend. We wandered another five hundred yards upstream to a spot where the underbrush was flattened and small trees uprooted. We sometimes find areas like this when a bull moose is in rut and paws the ground and rakes his antlers against trees to remove the velvet.

This area seemed very promising so we walked around in a widening circle till we came upon a large pile of leaves and twigs.

When we scraped away some of the overburden to see what was underneath we uncovered the remains of a yearling moose, partly decomposed and covered with maggots. We knew this was a bear kill - a grizzly bear kill! At the time there was a local story around the Edson area of a famous bear called "the Tom Hill grizzly," that achieved prominence when about five years previously three American hunters had lost two horses to this bear. Myles and I looked at each other, wondering if perhaps this was the same bear! We headed back to camp as we realized there would be no moose or elk in the area with a bear roaming around.

We broke camp, loaded up the 4-wheel drive and headed back towards town. While we were driving, it occurred to me that we could fly somewhere and do some hunting. Myles agreed and suggested a place called Sundance Lake - a narrow lake, not very long and located in the east slopes of the Canadian Rockies near Grande Cache, Alberta. We drove to where I was now keeping my aircraft at a farmer's dock on Long Lake as the campground at Bear Lake was closed for the season. We arrived there at dusk and after we refueled the plane we decided we would wait until morning to fly to Sundance Lake. We took the gear out and slept in the back of the truck under the canopy.

We flew out the next morning. When we arrived at the lake it was hard to see from the air as it was in a very deep canyon with only one way in and one way out. I had to fly along the creek running out of the lake and lower the altitude till the sides of the cliffs loomed high above the wing tips. I knew there was only one chance at an approach due to the deep canyon walls, once we are over the water there was no place to turn around. Myles gripped his seat and the handle of the door and said in a low voice, "Are we going to make it."

"I hope so," I replied.

The end of the lake was coming up just as the floats touched the water. We skipped once then the pontoons settled into the crystal green, glacial waters. After we'd unloaded the plane and set up camp we walked along the shoreline, Myles going one way and I the other. Suddenly Myles called out, "Ken, come over here. I found something." I ran along the shore to where he was and there hoisted up in the bush was a large freighter canoe with Northwest Pulp and Paper stamped on its side. Under it was a set of paddles. Now that we had a canoe to fish and hunt from we were set.

During the night we heard moose calling all night long. I answered with my birch bark moose horn. When they responded it sounded like they were right next to our camp. The way the noise echoed up and down the canyon we thought they were answering their own calls. Nervous on account of our bear encounter the day before, we got up and built a big fire.

Morning found the lake smothered in fog. When we climbed up a bank to see above it, it looked like white cotton batting covering the water.

Overhead, the sky was blue and sunlight was lighting up the tops of the canyon so we knew that once the sun warmed the valley the fog would burn off. We came down and climbed into the canoe. Myles decided to paddle first and I sat in the bow to be able to shoot if something came into view. We slid along under the mist, but the fog was so thick we couldn't see the shoreline. Myles tried calling a moose, and within a few minutes there was an answer just in front of us. We heard some splashing in the water, then nothing. He was using a J stroke to keep the canoe in line with me and the noise of the moose in the water'.

Gradually, the mist cleared a bit and a few trees became visible, then the shoreline. I chambered a 130-grain bullet into the barrel of my rifle, shouldered it and braced my feet along the sides of the canoe. The mist continued to lift enough that I thought I saw something in the water, but I wasn't sure.

I did see something. It was a big black stump. I looked again and there behind a stump on the shore was a large bull moose. I waited until I had the crosshairs centered on his breast and slowly squeezed the trigger. The valley shuttered from the blast and the canoe rocketed sideways. Myles brought the bow around and I fired another shot just as the mist came down and obscured the shore. We waited till the fog had cleared before we went to ashore, but we couldn't see or hear any trace of the moose. We searched around the shoreline until twenty-five feet in front of us we saw the moose. He had made it to a grassy patch before he lay down and died.

Now the real work began. Dressing out a moose is nothing but hard work. Three hours later we had the animal skinned and quartered and the meat wrapped in cheesecloth and hung in a tree to cool. Shortly after we had our animal dressed out we thought we heard a shot. Then we heard what sounded like the whining noise of a vehicle stuck in the mud. Curious, we paddled around the edge of the lake, fishing as we went along.

Around a point of land, there standing on the shore were two hunters. They had driven in with an old 4-wheel drive with large tires, and were now firmly stuck in the muskeg. They also had shot a moose, but they had a real problem. All they had to dress the animal out with was a small skinning knife. We dug out our knives, saws and axes and proceeded to help dress their kill. We also had a come-a-long, a hand-operated winch which we normally use to haul a moose out of the bush. We used the winch to pull the truck out of the muskeg. After we finished dressing the moose and the truck was pulled out of the mud, the hunters decided to celebrate with some Alberta Sipping Whiskey that came in a small wooden box. We sat around telling fishing and hunting stories till all the whiskey was gone, then Myles and I headed back to our camp.

Our next problem was to figure out how we were going to fly the moose out. We finally decided the only way to get all the meat out was to drain off some fuel into our Jerry cans so we could reduce the weight for take off, and make two or three trips back to Long Lake. With less gas I would be able to carry more of the moose meat out on one trip. I made several trips from Sundance Lake to Long Lake, leaving Myles with only the bare necessities while I flew back and forth

On October 10, 1981 I made my last flight out with Myles. As we plowed through the bulrushes and small willows, trying to gain altitude along the creek, Myles laughed nervously and said this was a flight he would never forget. As it turned out, this trip was very special for me as well as it was the last time I flew HDN on floats.

Chapter 18

There are many psychological factors at play when flying in the wilderness. On one such occasion "my friend, who I will call George," had flown into Caribou Lake in early November to hunt woodland Caribou. Because my aircraft was on skis I could land on most of the small lakes if they had six to twelve inches of ice on them. I needed at least six inches or more to land safely. With skis on I could carry much more weight in the aircraft than on floats, but I needed sufficient ice underneath to withstand the weight and pressure on the ice during take off. In early winter the ice actually rolls out in front of the aircraft during take off, almost like a wave.

When we flew over the south end of Caribou Lake we could see many tracks in the fresh snow. It is very difficult to tell a female from a male caribou as both have antlers. Flying along the edge of the lake we saw several caribou and decided to land some distance away from the animals we had seen.

After landing, we put on our snowshoes and walked along the shoreline till the animals were in range. We could see they all had wonderful racks of antlers. We picked out two bulls that were standing alone, some distance from the rest of the herd, and you can tell the difference between the male and female, because of the sex gear they carry. Even if they wear the same headdress. We decided to shoot at the same time so we didn't spook the rest of the herd. We fired twice at the animals; one went down, then the other. When we got to them we saw that they had the most amazing racks of antlers. We dressed them out and wrapped the quarters in cheesecloth. I went back and got the aircraft and taxied across the lake to where George waited with the animals. We removed the front seat and placed it on the shore. Then I spread heavy-gauge plastic sheeting in the backseat area and along the passenger seat area. I checked the weight of each quarter and felt that I could fly out with three quarters, but not a whole animal.

After some discussion we decided I would make two trips out, taking the heaviest quarters first and then make the last trip out with George and two small quarters. We built a nice fire on the shore, and set up the tarp using some trees to make a lean two. This provided shelter and warmth and a place to stay while I was flying the meat out.

When I returned from the first trip out, it seemed that my George was not comfortable about being alone in the bush. He didn't say much, but he indicated that he would like to go out on the second trip and leave the meat for me to take out later.

This didn't make much sense as we had already taken the passenger seat out so I could carry more meat. He was visibly upset and agitated, so I sat with him and had a cup of coffee and asked him if he was scared or what was bothering him. He replied "Nothing really, I just don't like it here." The meat was already loaded in the aircraft so there was nothing to do but assured him I would be back in about an hour. With that he threw more logs on the fire, and as I took off I saw him sitting on the aircraft seat gazing into the flames.

It took a little longer to get back than I had anticipated because I had to refuel, store the meat in the hanger then drive back to the lake where the aircraft was situated, as there was no ski runway close to the hanger. When I returned to Caribou Lake it was almost dark and I could see the fire burning on the shoreline. I landed and taxied over to the camp, shut the aircraft off and walked to where my partner was standing on the ice. He had a blank stare on his face, looking around the shoreline with his rifle in his hand. He just stood there staring across the lake and repeating over and over "The wolves, can you see them?"

I replied, "No, I can't," scanning the lake to see what he

was looking at, but I saw nothing. I had seen some on the lake when I was landing, but I couldn't see any from where we were. Then he said, "Can you hear them? Can you hear them?"

I replied, "Yes I can, but they are on the far side of the lake." I could see that he was very emotionally disturbed. I had him sit in the pilot's seat until I had the other two quarters loaded, then I installed the passenger seat and covered the meat with the excess plastic.

Given his condition, I unloaded his rifle and placed it in the rear of the aircraft. He was so disturbed I had to half carry him around to the passenger side of the aircraft. Although he had a rifle, food, and shelter, he had become very disoriented, and had become paranoid about being alone on the lake. It was almost dark now as I taxied the aircraft towards the animal carcasses and I saw three wolves feeding on the entrails. When I switched on my landing light, we saw their eyes reflecting menacingly in the darkness. George reached over and grabbed my arm. "Let's get the hell out of here!" And we did.

He was never the same again, and every time we went flying I had to make sure he had company with him. I took him fishing one more time about one hundred miles from home where we stayed in a lovely cabin along the shore of a lake. The first night we were there he went to the outhouse and thought he heard something in the bush. He became so agitated I had to fly him home. Not a little while, but right then, I never realized at the time how being alone in the wilderness could have such a profound effect on some people. However, since then this has happened on several occasions with several different people. Some were seasoned hunters and guides; with others it was just their first time in the wilderness. I have learned that once the mind and senses shift into high gear, and your imagination gets unleashed, you can imagine the worst things possible. The only people who never seem to be bothered about being alone in the bush are trappers and prospectors. In fact, they are much more at home in remote areas than living in the city.

The other thing that can happen when in a life-and-death situation is that people may see their life pass before them. On one such occasion I was flying on floats with zero visibility and unable to see the ground. The passenger I had with me started to talk continuously, almost like a confession. While I was trying to locate water to land on, or even a break in the clouds, he just kept talking. My main concern at the moment was not to die in this aircraft. His main concern was to get off his chest the many things that had been bothering him for the last twenty years. We had a conflict of interest: I wanted to live, and he didn't care whether he did or not.

I assured him that everything would be okay. Even though I was unable to see the ground. I told him we would talk about his situation after we had landed, even though I wasn't sure how we were going to land. He just kept talking, faster and faster. He told me what was wrong with his love life, his marriage, and how much he loved his children.

At last, when we broke through the last layer of clouds we were only about sixty feet above the ground. When I noticed a small lake to my starboard side and landed, while he was still talking. I know more things about this man's life then he would have revealed to a psychiatrist or a priest. It has been my experience that most stories have a profound effect on one's life including hearing them, not just telling them.

I had always thought I was immune to the effects of Mother Nature and the elements, but reality was about to take a small bite of my ass. Maybe a bigger bite than I anticipated.

Walter Penko, Ron Crone, and I were hunting on the Chinchaga River in northern Alberta. We had taken a boat downriver approximately ten miles, and had set up a base camp there when the weather took a sudden change and we were enveloped in a winter snowstorm. Not a small storm. It sent down two feet of wet sticky snow that collapsed our tent and made the river impassable. It snowed for twenty-four hours straight and everything was wet. We had no dry clothes and the only part of our bodies that was dry was what our hip waders covered.

We knew we couldn't get the boat or the tent out, so we decided to walk out and come back with skidoos and pack our gear out later. We were hoping that the highway wasn't as far as we thought it might be. Because the river meanders back and forth, distances were deceiving. After some discussion, we decided to walk the shortest distance in a straight line back to the highway. I had been walking behind Ron for about three miles when my mind began to wander; I decided I didn't need my backpack any more even though it contained dry clothes, food, and precious chocolate bars. So I hung it up in a spruce tree where I could pick it up on our return trip. I had been wet and cold since the previous day, and had had little sleep because the tent had collapsed on top of us, and walking through two feet of snow with hip waders on which isn't the best mode of transportation. We were approximately to what I thought was halfway to the highway when in my great wisdom I decided I didn't need my rifle anymore either. I hung it up in a spruce tree as well. Not too smart! But I had convinced myself all that I required was the waterproof matches that were in a container in my pocket.

I knew we were getting pretty close to the road when I thought I heard trucks using their jake brakes to gear down for the long hill to the river. But I wasn't sure if this was really what I heard as I had started to hear many things that weren't there - or maybe they were there. It was then I decided to have a little snooze. I tried to find a large spruce tree with overhanging branches and a dry patch at the base with leaves and needles to make a bed. Because the snow had fallen straight down, the large trees had gathered snow on their branches, leaving a dry pocket at the base of the tree. I crawled under one such tree, wrapped my arms around the trunk and slowly dropped off to sleep. Fortunately, my good friend Ron Crone noticed I was no longer behind him. He circled back on my tracks, which led him to my nice spruce lair. Although he was tired and wet himself, he wasn't about to abandon his friend. He jabbed me with his walking stick and said, "Ken get up, don't go to sleep or you'll never wake up."

I knew this was true, but I didn't seem to care. He got me up and made me walk in front of him. In about an hour wet, exhausted and very cold, we arrived at the road and found our Land Rover. We got out of our wet clothes and put on some dry coveralls that were in the back of the vehicle. We started the engine and turned the heater up to high, not caring if we ran out of fuel as we had spare fuel in a Jerry can. I stretched out on the back seat, while Ron slept in the front seat next to Walter. We were warm, safe, and dry and alive and that's all that mattered. We slept for over three hours, ate some chocolate bars, and drove home to High Level.

The following week, we returned with two skidoos and recovered the boat, tent, rifles and backpack.

Chapter 19

The last chapter should be the easiest, but I found it to be the most difficult. I feel that I have come to the end of a book that I have been working on for the past twelve years. This would be a relief to most people, but it is also an end to a part of my life, a life in which most of my dreams have come true.

In the latter part of my flying career, I usually took people up over the mountains west of Jasper, Alberta. On this particular trip, I took Myles with me on a night flight over Mount Robson, the highest mountain in the Canadian Rockies. It is 12,972 feet above sea level; it is located just west of Jasper on Highway 16. If you view this mountain from the highway you will notice there is a small notch at the very top of the mountain.

Myles and I took off from Edson one night, flew over Jasper and continued on to Mt. Robson. I required an altitude of approximately 15,000 feet to fly over the top of the mountain. It was a brilliant evening, with a full moon and stars dancing in the sky. I made my first pass over the mountain and peered out the side window to get a better view of the glaciers and the craggy top. I decided to turn out all the aircraft lights, both inside and out, so we could get a better view of the mountain. In the pitch black cabin the snow-covered mountains seemed so close as if we could have actually reached out and touched them.

The Canadian Rockies just west of Jasper in the moonlight

Myles and Ken flying over Mount Robson these photos were taking using moonlight only

This gave me an idea. I would lose some altitude, slow the aircraft down and fly through the notch at the top of the mountain. As we approached the mountain, Myles' hands grabbed the side of his seat and held on tightly. Soon we were inside the mountain with the rocky ramparts looming in each window, and we were considerably lower than we should have been. I slowed the aircraft down even more and aimed for the opening on the far side of the mountain. With the moon reflecting off the snow-topped mountains, the view was spectacular. The depths of the snow banks varied from two to three hundred feet deep. The wind blew wisps of snow over the aircraft, slightly obscuring our vision. Myles hands tightened a little more on the side of his seat when we flew through the notch and came out the other side. Far below us was Highway 16 where we could see the occasional vehicle moving. Flying home to Edson, I knew in my heart this was the best night flight I had ever had, or would ever be likely to have.

Flying from Mount Robson over the town site of Jasper Alberta

On May 30th 1983, I flew to High Level to have the annual inspection done on my aircraft. Ziggy Wojciechowski, another pilot from the Edson Flying Club came with me. The return trip to Edson was the last time I ever flew my CF-HDN again.

On April 6, 1984 I crossed over to the Other Side, but I didn't stay there very long. I came back or I wouldn't have been here to write about my flying experiences. That was the day I suffered a major heart attack, but the good part about it is that I had the good fortune to have been in the Royal Inland Hospital in Kamloops, British Columbia at the time. I had been sent to the Kamloops hospital to have some blood work done. I was awakened about one o'clock in the morning with the most excruciating pain I have ever experienced. My chest felt like someone had hit me with an axe. I sat straight up in bed, pressed the call button and fell back on the bed.

The next recollection I had was of sitting on the little table that the meals are served on, watching and listening to the crash cart team while they administered drugs, intravenous lines and many other goodies. I couldn't believe my eyes. I was sitting watching and listening to people trying to save my life! I had the most wonderful sense of joy and peace that is very hard to describe. I heard people talking, and there seemed to be a general consensus among the group that I wasn't going to make it. I'm not a very religious man even though I did teach Sunday school at one time, but that was it. Yes, I did see the "blue light" one hears about in the stories of near death experiences, but to me it was actually a blue, white and lavender-colored light. In the room I sensed a feeling of serenity, and this gave me the most contented feeling I had ever had in my life. So, if I was looking through my soul to the body that was lying on the bed, I've been there! Of course, this gave me a new aspect to flying, which I had always thought was the ultimate high. But now I know it doesn't get any better than what I experienced that day.

The only communication we had at the lake was a point-to-point radio. I heard the doctor telling Helen that the next forty-eight hours would be the most critical. He told her not to come in until the following morning. I could hear the sound of panic and fear in her voice. As they had her on a speaker phone, but there was nothing I could do to comfort her.

When I regained consciousness in the intensive care ward I was only semiconscious, but you have no idea how aggravating it is to listen to your own heartbeat coming from the monitor above your bed. I suppose it's supposed to be a reassuring sound.

When I was discharged from the hospital I was told I had to make some major lifestyle changes to reduce stress, I would have to exercise more, and I would have take a lot of pills. Since then I've read many books on near death experiences and oxygen deprivation, written by people who believe in it and those that don't. I can only relate my own experience

Because of my heart attack I lost my medical clearance, so I was prevented from flying. I wasn't sure if I could even work again, but after three months of recuperation, I passed my medical and was back on the job again. The psychological effect of reviewing my own mortality changed the way I looked at things in life. Many of the things I had thought were important had no significant value, and things like family and friends went to the top of the list.

I sold my aircraft in the spring of 1984. The only good thing about that was that it went north to Anchorage, Alaska where there were lots of lakes, mountains, tundra, and muskeg to make my old bird feel right at home. I couldn't help but miss my dear airplane, as it had been a part of my life for many years.

In the spring of 1986, the International Cessna 170 Association ran an Article on my airplane, the Cessna 170B, with a picture of Helen standing beside it. We had just completely painted the aircraft in 1973, and we thought it was one of the most beautiful planes we had ever seen. This aircraft was built in 1954, and serial number of the aircraft was 25922.

Today I'm still flying, but I have been moved into the position of copilot and navigator, but this year in 2006, my medical doctor informed me, that I might be able to get my medical aviation certificate.

In closing, I would like to share with you some words that another pilot composed in 1941.

In December 1941, pilot Officer John G. Magee, a 19-year-old American serving with the Royal Canadian Air Force in England, was killed when his Spitfire collided with another aircraft inside a cloud. Several months before his death, he composed an immortal sonnet "High Flight" a copy that he fortunately mailed to his parents in the USA and that goes like this:

Oh, I have slipped the surly bonds of earth.
And danced the skies on laughter silvered wings;
Sunward I've climbed, and join the tumbling mirth.
Of sun split clouds and done a hundred things.
You have not dreamed of wheeled and soared and swung
High in the sunlit silence, hovering there,
I've chased the shouting wind along, and flung
My eager craft through footless halls of air,
Up, up the long delirious, burning blue.
I've talked the wind swept heights with easy grace.
Were never lark, or even an eagle flew.
And, while with silent, lifting mind. I've trod
The high untresspassed sanctity of space,
Put out my hand, and touched the face of God.
-- *John Gillespie Magee, Jr.*

The End

Notes